THE  *Map*

THE *Map*

TO OUR
RESPONSIVE
UNIVERSE—
WHERE DREAMS
REALLY DO
COME TRUE!

BONI LONNSBURRY

Inner Art Inc.
1750 30th Street, Suite 543
Boulder, CO 80301

www.innerartinc.com

Editor: Colleen Mauro
Cover Design: *the*Bookdesigners
Interior Graphics: Devon Gibbs

Ordering Information:

Quantity sales. Special discounts are available on quantity purchases by corporations, associations, and others. For details, contact the publisher at the address above.

Publisher's Cataloging-in-Publication data

Lonnsburry, Boni.
    The map to our responsive universe — where dreams really do come true! / Boni Lonnsburry.
      p. cm.
      ISBN 978-0-9890594-3-5
      Includes index.

1. New thought. 2. Self realization (psychology). 3. Success. 4. Joy. 5. Optimism. 6. Metaphysics.
I. Title.

BF639 .L79 2013
131 --dc23   pcngoeshere

For Richard –
the most amazing magician I know.

CONTENTS

Introduction.. 1

Chapter One: The Art of Conscious Creation........... 11

Chapter Two: Follow the Map to a Life You Love 27

Chapter Three: Who *Are* You, Really? 47

Chapter Four: Clarifying Your Dream 61

Chapter Five: Bringing Your Dream to Life! 107

Chapter Six: The 24/7 Flow: Beliefs 147

Chapter Seven: Techniques to Increase the Flow..... 203

Chapter Eight: Action: Accelerating the Process...... 229

Chapter Nine: Your Reality Will Respond 253

Chapter Ten: The Secret to Faster Change 289

Chapter Eleven: Make Room for Miracles 305

Chapter Twelve: Changing Your Life 317

Index 339

Appendix A: Building a Dream From the Ashes 343

Appendix B: A Letter From Your Future Self 355

Appendix C: Requests to Your Higher Self............. 359

INTRODUCTION

"You are given the gift of the gods;
you create your reality according to your beliefs;
yours is the creative energy that makes your world;
there are no limitations to the self except those you believe in."

—SETH

You create your own reality. No fine print. No exceptions. No asterisks.

I can't imagine anyone reading those words and *not* being excited!

You...did you get that? Are you letting that in?

YOU CREATE YOUR OWN REALITY!

Yes. Really. ALL of it!

All the joy, all the love, all the successes are your creations. All the misery, all the scarcity, all the struggle are also *your* creations. OK, maybe you aren't conscious of *how* you have created it—yet—but it is still your creation. And if *it is* your creation, the difficulties in your life aren't because of your parents, or spouse, or children, or the economy, or the politicians, or your body, or your boss.

And that is great news. If no one other than you is to blame, *you* are the one with the power.

If everything in your life *is* your creation you can become *conscious* of that creation and *change* it. You can learn how to *consciously create* joy, abundance, love, fun and ease.

Can you imagine a world where *everyone* felt empowered to create a life they loved? Can you imagine a world where people were free to choose—and then manifest—the most joyous life possible?

If everything is indeed our creation, then it's not only our immediate lives that can change. *We can also create a different world.*

I don't know about you, but the thought of having the power to impact my world is amazing to me.

I am not here to convince anyone of the fact that we create it all. There are plenty of books out there on quantum physics that scientifically prove the premise. I am here to work with those of you who know, on some level, that you are a God-being, complete with an inherent ability to create.

And I'm here to share what I've learned during my journey, to hopefully make yours easier.

WHAT IS THE MAP?

I have worked with the principles of conscious creation for nearly three decades. I have studied and worked with dozens, if not hundreds, of teachers, authors, healers and channeled entities. I have learned from each of them and I believe they each had their gifts for me.

I have scoured my conscious and subconscious minds for what caused my most disappointing and painful realities, as well as the most successful and triumphant ones. I have painstakingly broken down each and every area of my life, and bit by bit, built it back the way I wanted it.

And when I couldn't find a tool to make it easier to manifest my reality in accordance with my dreams, I invented my own. I invented the "Map."

The Map is a process of conscious creation. It begins with knowing who you are. And it ends with you knowing you are unconditionally loved and that huge amounts of assistance are available to you.

The Map is a step-by-step guide on "how to create." The Map will help you to build a dream, whether you know what you want or not.

It will help you to bring those dreams alive by showing you how to flow energy towards those dreams and even more importantly, it will show you how to *stop* flowing energy towards your nightmares.

The Map then guides you as to *what to do in the world* to support that dream. And The Map explains precisely how to know if what you are doing is working. And even more critical...what to do if it's *not*.

The Map is, quite simply, a step-by-step *dream making machine*.

WHAT HAS THE MAP DONE FOR ME?

I HAVE USED THIS PROCESS TO CREATE FINANCIAL ABUNDANCE.

I was born into a family that struggled financially and I didn't do much better as a young adult. Unable to break out of the scarcity mindset, I found myself facing foreclosure in my early forties. I declared bankruptcy. I seriously wondered who might take me in if I were homeless.

I hit bottom financially. And I applied The Map. Not that many years later, money has ceased to be an issue.

I now enjoy a life most people cannot imagine for themselves. I live in a home overlooking the Rocky Mountains of Boulder, Colorado, with unbelievable city views at night and spectacular mountain views in the daytime.

And when Boulder is too chilly, I live in an equally spectacular home on the ocean in the Bahamas. I travel back and forth in a private jet, which allows an elegance and ease to a lifestyle that could be hectic and burdensome.

I have used this Map to create a five-million-dollar business with only a fifty-dollar investment. Finding myself jobless and uncertain as to what to do, I followed The Map and surprisingly (even to me) doors repeatedly opened to allow an amazing and totally fun creation.

My partner and I each spent fifty dollars to incorporate In Touch Today—a marketing company that created direct mail products for mortgage and real estate professionals.

A few months later, I bought my partner out, and never put in another dollar. Deciding that fun was the most important thing, I created a company that was great fun to work for, be around and do business with. I seldom worked past five o'clock, took vacations often and decided that if I didn't love it, I would hire someone else to do it.

The philosophy (and following The Map) paid off. The company organically grew and I ran it for twelve years before selling it on the last day of 2011.

I HAVE USED THE MAP TO CREATE A DEEPLY LOVING RELATIONSHIP.

Relationships had also been challenging for me, yet I yearned to experience a deeply loving partnership, within which I felt a sense of peace, safety, fun, freedom, ease, joy, intimacy, vulnerability and trust.

Prior to my current relationship, I had been an expert at *attracting* men into my life, but invariably there was something missing or there was a major disconnect in a core value between us.

The Map was my guide, and I applied it, time and again, over and over. With each relationship I learned more about myself and why I attracted the men I did. I changed belief after belief and moved ever closer to my dream.

Finally, with nothing (self-imposed) stopping me, I met and ultimately married my "dream come true." And yes, he was worth waiting for (read...working my butt off for!).

I HAVE USED THE MAP TO CREATE A VITAL, YOUTHFUL AND HEALTHY BODY.

Health, vitality, well being and regression of aging...they are all possible and creatable *if* you *believe* they are. By applying The Map, I have been able to heal disease and injuries in a gentle and (mostly) holistic way and I continue to experience (aka create) the health and body I desire.

I HAVE USED THE MAP TO CREATE A RELATIONSHIP WITH MY CHILDREN THAT ALLOWS THEM TO BE FREE AND EMPOWERED TO LIVE THE LIVES THEY REALLY LOVE.

My sons were a major test of my creative abilities. As children and teens, they faced challenge after challenge—health, drugs, depression and more. What's a parent to do?

Apply The Map. I sought to understand *my* part in my children's problems. I am not saying their issues were my fault. I am saying my attachment to whether or not they were healed, happy and whole, paradoxically kept them from finding their wholeness, healing and happiness. Applying The Map helped me to end the codependency. It works. And it is still working.

I HAVE USED THE MAP TO REMAIN IN STATES OF JOY AND HAPPINESS, AND TO KNOW WHAT TO DO WHEN I SLIP OUT OF THOSE STATES.

I was an emotional basket case in my teen and early adult years. Forever seeking change, growth, creativity and joy, I was perpetually disappointed and often spent my evenings in tears.

I just didn't know how to make things happen. And when I found out how our world *really* works, life finally made sense, even if I had no skill (yet) to actually change my reality.

But eventually I figured it out. I learned *how* to consciously create my reality and I got better and better at it and had more and more reasons to be happy.

However, ultimately happiness is still a *choice*. And although The Map *did* teach me how to empower myself, it also taught me how to spend more and more time in that delicious state of joy, no matter what happened in the world around me.

ULTIMATELY...

I have used The Map to create a life I adore. Am I perfect? No, I am not. Is my life perfect? Absolutely not. It is a work in progress and something that is unfinished is never perfect.

But it *is* a life that is perfect for *me*. And when issues *do* arise, when something happens in my life that is *not* to my liking, I know what to do to shift my reality. *That* is empowerment.

WHAT CAN THE MAP DO FOR YOU?

If you follow it, The Map can not only help you to discover and clarify your dreams, it can help you to make them manifest in your world—in vivid, delightful, synchronistic and fulfilling ways.

With The Map, you will follow a clear, concise and step-by-step process to make your dreams real. You will learn how to tell if it is working. You will also learn what to do if it doesn't work. And even if you need more help, guidance or healing outside of this Map, The Map will show you how to draw that help into your life.

I wanted my successes to be duplicate-able. That is why I spent so many years perfecting what I know about reality creation. And now *you* can reap the rewards of my perseverance.

Again, there are no exceptions to "you create it all," folks. You came here to create a life of your dreams. I *know* you can do this. **It is what you came to do.**

WHY I WROTE THIS BOOK

I write, blog and teach seminars on how to create your own reality because I find conscious reality creation the most exciting thing on the planet to ponder, discuss, apply and teach. I *love* the way this works. I love that it *does* work. And I love the fact that when we become empowered by living the life we love, we can't help but raise the vibration of all that is, spreading more empowerment, more freedom and more love.

Everything I have ever dreamed of has come true. And the next part of my dream is dreaming a world that has more people feeling empowered, excited and passionate about their lives. A world that has more people living a life they love.

I wrote this book to provide more direction. Time and again people have asked me for a step-by-step guide to create what they want. This is it.

So let's get started. There is no time like the present to live a life you love!

In joyous creation,

ONE

THE ART OF CONSCIOUS CREATION

*"You cannot teach a man anything, you can
only help him learn it within himself."*

—GALILEO

We have been living in darkness on this planet. Few have discovered the fact that we *do* create our own realities and fewer have applied it successfully to all areas of their lives. What makes this concept even more confusing is that many have written and spoken about it in half-truths.

These half-truths have left many feeling that they *know* the truth about how life works. Yet when they look at their lives after applying these "truths," they are disappointed because nothing really changes.

Therefore, I want to start by explaining what I *don't* mean when I say "you create it all."

HERE'S WHAT I'M NOT TALKING ABOUT:

I am not talking about "changing your perspective" and reframing bad news as "good," although if you do create lemons you might as well make lemonade. But for goodness sake, if you can stop creating the lemons in the first place, isn't that a better choice?

I am also not talking about giving up desire and being "happy with what you have." However, I strongly believe in the power of gratitude.

I am not even talking about the "power of positive thinking." Of course being positive helps, but it is just a small piece of a very large pie.

I am certainly not talking about living only for the future and not enjoying each and every "now" moment.

And believe me, *I am not talking about* "turning your life over to God" and trusting that whatever shows up is "meant to be," even though I absolutely believe in a divine power and His/Her ability to love us unconditionally and assist in our creations.

But this is a planet of free will, folks. And God has a hands-off policy (unless invited or in dire circumstance) because *we set it up that way*. We came to this world of illusion to prove our power to ourselves! Then (and only then) do we begin to co-create with God and Goddess.

It is the half-truths that delude, disappoint and leave us feeling powerless and hopeless. But there is a light of awakening growing within many of us. And you are reading this book because somehow, in some way, you *know* there is more to the story. You also know, on some level, that you have more ability to create than you have ever imagined possible.

WHAT "CONSCIOUSLY CREATING YOUR OWN REALITY" *DOES* MEAN:

Consciously creating your reality means you can take one hundred percent responsibility for all areas of your life and your world. You can change your world *substantively*.

You can change your financial abundance, love life, health and vitality, career/work, relationships, physical surroundings, creativity, emotional well-being and every other aspect of your life imaginable.

Your life can be more than you have ever dreamed. I am not talking about the trappings—the cars, the money, the career, the spouse—although they *will* come if you allow them to. I am talking about the deep meaning life can offer—the joy, the ecstasy even, and yes, the fun!! Life should be loads of fun, and so much more.

And once you take responsibility for *your own* life, and empower yourself to create a life you love, you can then begin to have impact on the lives of others—and on the *world*.

You can only imagine so far right now; yet at the edge of your imagination (imagining the best your life can get) lives another you, who *has* that life.

Let's call that "you" a future you—and that future you isn't finished dreaming. That future you has dreams you cannot yet imagine. Imagine that!

Will those be dreams of more cars, money and things? Probably not...you can only have so many of those things before it gets boring (really).

The future you will be dreaming of more love, joy, fun, meaning, creativity, connectedness and a planet that has those beautiful energies in spades. Imagine *that*!

Everyone has the ability to create a life they love. Everyone. Some are not ready for this news yet. Some have more pressing issues to deal with, such as surviving day to day. But if you are reading this, you *are* ready.

Please know this: as long as you are human, you will have dreams. You will never be done dreaming or creating. The specifics will change. Your *dreams* as a twenty-year-old will be different from your dreams as an eighty-year-old, but you will always *desire more.*

And creating this illusion we live in will never be finished. As long as you are alive you will be creating your reality because this is the way the world works. And if you are not *consciously* creating it, you will be *unconsciously* creating it.

And you'll like the results better if you participate consciously.

WHAT'S THE CATCH?

Consciously creating your reality does not mean you can control what it looks like when it manifests.

What? But that is precisely what I want to control!

I disagree. There may be an aspect of you that wants to control the way it looks, but the higher aspects of your being primarily want the *emotional* outcome...the feelings of prosperity, love, joy, fulfillment, etc. And quite honestly, that is the *only* part you can control.

What about the things? The lovers, husband, wife, job, house, money, etc.?

Nope. Those are *side effects.* Yes, they show up when you focus on your life in a certain way. But they are not the objective. The objective is to *feel* a certain way about certain areas of your life.

Think about it. There are plenty of people who have tons of money but it's never enough...they are never satisfied, never secure and they never feel truly abundant.

There are people who have the spouse, but not the trust, the support, the respect and the ever-deepening love.

There are people who have careers that they thought would make them happy, but they don't feel free, creative and excited and they aren't having fun.

The *things* are not what bring you the essence (the wonderful, positive feeling states). The essence (the wonderful positive feelings states) is what brings you the *things.*

So when you consciously create, in order to have that scrumptious essence, that delicious life, you must let go of how it will look. Believe me, you'll be a thousand times happier if you do.

THE UPSIDE IS…

If you really follow The Map of conscious creation, outlined in chapter two, you will end up with a life that is far *better than you could have imagined even* if *you* could *control every tiny detail.*

Let *that* in.

MY "BEST OF EVERYTHING" CREATION

When I let go of control, I am amazed at how well things turn out. Not that it's always easy to do…believe me it isn't. But when I do manage it, my life works so much better than when I try to make things turn out in a certain way.

For example, a few years back, I was thinking about this lifetime being my last one on earth (I'm pretty sure it is, however I reserve the right to change my mind!).

I thought about all the great creations (i.e., the art, books, movies, etc.) on this planet that I hadn't yet experienced, as well as the beautiful places in nature that I hadn't seen, and decided then and there, that in my remaining years, I wanted to experience the "best of everything" I could.

I didn't decide what that would look like. I just decided that in whatever way I could, I would open to the gifts to be found on this planet.

I began by downloading a list of the top one hundred novels of all time, according to a survey of librarians. And I started reading the books.

I also downloaded a list of the one hundred greatest movies of all time according to *Time* magazine. And I began watching the movies.

I really didn't give the dream of experiencing the "best of everything" much more thought. But the universe sure delivered.

I had never owned a passport prior to declaring this dream (and honestly travel wasn't even in my remotest thoughts), but only five years later, I not only have a passport, but it is full!

I have seen some of the most beautiful places on the planet, stayed in five-star hotels, sailed on private yachts, visited the most highly regarded spas and eaten in some of the best restaurants in the *world*.

All I can say is that I'm glad I didn't try to control *this* dream. I would've settled for just reading the one hundred best books and watching the one hundred greatest movies!

YOU MAY HAVE SOME RESISTANCE TO THESE WORDS

Human beings are resistant to change—even good change. Many of us are afraid to dream, afraid to hope because of a fear of failure and yes, a fear of success. We've been disappointed, disillusioned and beaten down. But this is because we've all been in the dark for so long.

What should you do if resistance comes up for you? Love the part of you that is afraid. How? Just by honoring its presence. Accept that you are a complex being, capable of a myriad of seemingly conflicting emotions all at once.

There is also a part of you that does not want to take responsibility. There is a part of you that will argue for your limitations. And there is likely a part of you that believes you are incapable, undeserving or unworthy of creating a life you love.

We all have those aspects. It's OK. I just want to point out that those parts will be there. If you feel conflicted and confused, be gentle and patient with yourself. Ask for clarity and direction from your higher self or God/Goddess or another unseen friend (more on exactly how to do that later in this book). Guidance will come.

WHAT DOES THIS REALLY MEAN FOR YOU?

I have no clue. I don't know you. I don't know your dedication to living a life you love.

Are you committed to living a life of your dreams, no matter how long it takes or how uncomfortable you become?

Do you have the courage to look at every one of your thoughts, emotions and beliefs to ferret out the ones that are creating what you *don't* want?

Do you have the perseverance to break down every aspect of your life, and rebuild it one piece at a time until your reality responds exactly the way you want?

I understand this may be daunting...and there are ways to look at your thoughts without monitoring every single one of them. But your dedication to this process will be instrumental in your success.

You won't be perfect at this. And it won't always be easy.

I have been repeatedly disappointed, disillusioned and heartbroken as I tried to create the perfect (for me) life. Not because the universe *didn't* deliver, but because it *did*. Every mis-creation came back to *me*. *My* energy was the culprit.

I jumped headfirst into a career in teaching and speaking on this very subject, but I didn't have the self-image to sustain it. I thought I could "create" getting rich quick with a multi-level marketing company, only to dig myself deeper and deeper in debt, due to my beliefs that didn't allow for easy, elegant abundance. I thought I'd met the man of my "dreams" not once, but five times, only to be bitterly disappointed that none of them lived up to my expectations.

Yeah, I cried. I fumed in my anger and self-pity. But once I *felt* the disappointment and *forgave* myself for creating what I did, I got back to work and did what it took to create a different outcome. Are you *that* dedicated?

I *know* that if you apply these principles, honestly and diligently, your life *will* change for the better. How much better is up to you.

This book may lead you to other resources, and it may not. The best advice I can give you is to follow your own heart and mind, follow the advice that feels right to you, and have fun with it all.

Growth, like life, is meant to be empowering and fun. (If you don't believe that, uh, maybe change that belief?)

If you're doubtful, no problem. A little doubt never hurt anyone. However if you're cynical, be careful. Cynicism will not serve you. If you want to convince yourself that you do not create your reality, that belief will *appear* to be true. This is powerful stuff. And it does work all the time.

The bottom line with this material and any other "how to" information is this: *Is your life changing for the better?*

If it is, don't stop until you're exquisitely happy with your entire life!

If your life *isn't* changing, ask yourself, why not? There is *always* a reason why our reality is the way it is. This is not a "sometimes" law.

Try following the steps in the book. Have fun with them. See what happens—after all, what do you have to lose?

MY EARLY YEARS

Prior to accepting this universal law, I felt lucky in many ways. I was born in a country with opportunity. I was healthy and intelligent. I had family and friends who cared about me.

But something was missing. Life didn't make sense. And when I looked around at the violence and hatred on our planet, and at the greed and obsession with power at any cost, it made even less sense.

I wondered, "*What is our reason for being here? If there is a God, where is He in all this? What kind of God would permit the atrocities that take place in our world?"* The lack of answers and meaning often left me feeling sad and depressed.

Then someone gave me a book on reincarnation by Edgar Cayce. I don't remember the title of the book, but I was so enthralled that I read every book Cayce wrote; and for the first time, I saw a glimmer of hope. The world started to make sense.

If our presence on this planet weren't simply an accident of some wild mutation of cosmic dust, then maybe human lives had purpose and meaning? I began to feel as if maybe *I* had purpose and meaning too.

That book led me to hundreds more on the topics of metaphysics and spirituality, but the most intriguing of all were the books on the nature of reality.

The first time I read the words, *"You create your own reality,"* I *knew* it was true. I felt like someone unlocked my jail cell. Of course I had no clue how to actually walk out of that cell and into a life I loved.

But that sense of knowing that it was *somehow possible* has kept me searching for the answer to *"how do I do this?"* for years. It kept me from giving up. It motivated me to let go of my safe and comfy complacency over and over again.

I keep coming back, even now, to the same core concept: *I create my own reality.*

The power of those words never fails to move me. And the sense of security I feel because of them is irrevocable; because if *I* created it, *no one* can take it away.

Even if I lost all the "things" in my life, through a bit of mis-creating, I would still be OK, because I can always create them *again*.

That is absolute empowerment.

LIFE-ALTERING TAKE AWAYS

Read these slowly. Meditate on them or sit and contemplate them. Let them in. Let them change you.

+ Consciously creating your reality means you can take one hundred percent responsibility for all areas of your life and your world. You can change your world *substantively*.

+ As long as you are alive you will be creating your reality because this is the way the world works. And if you are not *consciously* creating it, you will be *unconsciously* creating it.

+ Things will not bring you the essence (the wonderful, positive feeling states). The essence (the wonderful, positive feeling states) is what will bring you the things.

YOUR NEXT STEPS

☐ Purchase a journal to use as your Creation Journal or start a new document on your computer and name it Creation Journal. You will use this journal to document your intentions, techniques, actions, beliefs and successes as you do this work.

☐ I suggest that you revisit this journal often as a way to regain a sense of power, confidence and expectation. It is very effective to bring these energies to *new* dreams and visions. You accomplish this by simply reading about your past successes and feeling a sense of accomplishment and power before you do any techniques for your new dreams.

☐ Ponder what creating your own reality means to you. On a scale of one to ten, one *being, "I don't believe it is possible to create one's own reality at all,"* and ten *being, "I am certain every human on this planet is creating their own reality, and I have the absolute ability to consciously create everything in my own life,"* where are you? Where would you like to be in one year? In five years?

☐ Intend to get there. Suggested intention: *"I intend to know and fully believe—beyond a shadow of a doubt—that I create everything in my reality and that I can create a life of my dreams."*

TWO

FOLLOW THE MAP TO A LIFE YOU LOVE

"I read and walked for miles at night along the beach, writing bad blank verse and searching endlessly for someone wonderful who would step out of the darkness and change my life. It never crossed my mind that that person could be me."

—ANNA QUINDLEN

A LITTLE BACKGROUND:

There is a more *real* "you" who chose to come to this planet. That part of you wanted to experience certain things this lifetime. Before you were born you chose your parents, your siblings, the time and place of your birth and some of your childhood experiences. Obviously you also chose to forget just about everything you knew once you were born.

> You forgot that you were a God-being.
> You forgot that you chose to incarnate on a planet of free will.
> You forgot that "reality" is an illusion.
> You forgot that you create it all.
> You forgot that you are connected to everything everywhere.

Why did you do this? Because the thrill of remembering is so much fun. And because you thought this would be a good way to learn more about who you are.

HOW REALITY (AKA THE ILLUSION) IS CREATED:

Until you learn how to create what you desire *consciously*, you create your reality *unconsciously*. You are still creating your reality—but it seems random. It seems as if you are a victim of fate and circumstance, and that you can only move forward by determination, willpower or luck.

This is the way it *really* works: you attract things, people and experiences with the energy emitted by your thoughts, feelings and beliefs.

A thought, connected to feelings, along with beliefs, attracts your experiences in this world.

> Is health attracted (or repelled) into your life? Yes.
> Is money attracted (or repelled) into your life? Yes.
> Are relationships—good, bad or indifferent? Yes.
> Is success? Yes.
> Joy? Yes.
> Creativity? Yes.
> Freedom? Yes.
> Beauty? Yes.
> Love? Acceptance? Belonging? Yes. Yes. Yes.

YES! Whatever energy you put out there...good, bad or indifferent, the answer is...yes.

ARE THERE EXCEPTIONS?

Sometimes. But very few. And only if you chose them yourself before you began this lifetime. For instance, if you were born into this lifetime with a physical or mental challenge... a higher aspect of you may really *want* that experience and won't allow it to change.

And that is likely not you, and even if it were, you could change everything else in your world (and maybe even that too). So let's move on to how *do* you do it? How do you consciously create a life that is absolutely, positively the most *delicious* life you could live?

It is not difficult, folks. But it is a bit complex. Therefore it is critical to understand the complexities. Then and only then can you allow the grace that is "who you are" to consciously create a truly blissful life.

IT SOUNDS TOO EASY

What's the rub? Why isn't everyone creating a life they love?

Well, there are several reasons:

First, most of us aren't creating lives we love because we don't know *how*. Yet. But since this is the reason we become physical in the first place, you can bet your bottom dollar everyone *will* learn how at some point or another (granted, maybe not this lifetime).

Second, it is a bit more complex than "think a thought, pair it with a happy feeling" and voila! Success!

We are not one-dimensional beings. We are multi-dimensional beings. Our most deeply held beliefs play a big role in creating our reality—beliefs we may not be conscious of. So consciously creating a life you love takes some work.

Can you learn how? Absolutely. *If* you are dedicated to the process.

Is it worth it? Oh my God, yes! Yes, yes, a thousand times yes!!

Third, there is this little thing called *time lag*. Time lag is the time it takes for something to manifest in time and space. A thought and feeling you had two weeks ago could manifest in your reality today.

Meanwhile, you've forgotten all about what you thought, felt and said to a co-worker about the lack of good jobs out there. But the universe didn't forget, and today there is a *reason* you can't find any jobs worth applying for.

Time lag makes people believe what they see, instead of realizing that they see what they believe (and think and feel).

Conscious creation is a whole new way of life for almost every one of us. It took decades to get to where we are with the old way of life. Learning a new one takes some time and effort. But again, the results are worth it.

UNDERSTANDING THE BIG PICTURE— AN OVERVIEW OF THE MAP

When you look at a road map to plan a major trip, you don't begin by planning where to turn at the edge of your driveway. You step back, and look at the big picture first. If, for example, you plan to drive from New York City to Los Angeles, you would first choose the major highways, and then map out the smaller streets.

If you take a wrong turn here or there, the street signs will help you to adjust your route and get back on course. And you never lose sight of the big picture, the broad sweep of where you want to go.

The Map to our responsive universe will require the same skill set. First you'll look at the big picture—your overall dream. Then you'll break it down into small baby steps, so you can be certain to stay on course. And if you still happen to veer off track, you'll learn how to read the "signs" and adjust accordingly to head (once again) in the direction of your dreams.

STEP ONE: KNOW WHO YOU ARE.

You begin with you, and knowing who you (really) are.

This is a core concept.

We will come back to this knowing (remembering) time and time again. If this core knowing of who you are is not solid, you will find it hard to create what you desire.

I will teach you how to solidify this knowing. You will practice deepening this ownership of who you really are: a spark of God, of Goddess, of the Divine, and of All That Is.

STEP TWO: KNOW WHAT YOU WANT TO CREATE.

Think about this. Your thoughts, emotions and beliefs create your world.

Lets take that deeper. To create your world you need to put forth thoughts *and* emotions that are in *alignment with what you want*, and you have to *believe* it is possible.

So...bottom line. *What do you want?*

You need to know this, folks. Some will say they have no idea.

I would say...you always know *something*. Maybe you don't know what you *do* want... but you know what you *don't* want, right?

And you certainly know how you want to *feel*, right?

That's all you need. Really.

This book will help you to discover your *true* dreams. Not the dreams your parents, or spouse or society has for you.

The *only* dreams that will be truly fulfilling (and the ones that are most likely to manifest with ease) are those that speak to your heart and soul.

And once you have an idea of what it is you'd like to create you move on to...

STEP THREE: FLOWING ENERGY.

What does flowing energy mean? It means to focus positive thoughts and emotions on your dream.

The more you think about your desires with excitement, joy, expectation, delight, anticipation, wonder and triumph, the faster your dream will manifest. This is where the techniques come in.

From the easiest technique—simply reading your list of dreams (or intentions)—to the most involved, you need to flow energy to your dreams in order to make them manifest. It doesn't matter which technique you use as much as the fact that you *do* flow energy towards what you want.

And it is just as important to make sure that you are not *stopping* the flow of energy. You may be stopping it without even realizing it!

How does this happen?

Well, let's imagine that you want to create more money in your life, but you have a deeply held belief that says it is not possible for you to do that. Even though you may be flowing energy in the form of techniques to create more money, that belief is sending out its own flow of energy to bring you a *lack* of money. Like two forces in opposition, the strongest wins.

But no worries, anything can be changed. This is the phenomenal news! Everything that *isn't* working in your life can change! You *deserve* a life of your dreams. This is what you came here to live.

This step will focus on not only flowing energy, but discovering the deeply held beliefs that you don't even know are there, and *changing* them to be in alliance with (instead of in opposition to) your deepest desires. This...is reality changing.

So what happens after you have focused the flow of energy to be in alignment with your desires?

STEP FOUR: TAKE (INSPIRED) ACTION!

Actions *do* speak louder than words. Actions tell the universe that you are *serious* about having the things you want. They tell your subconscious mind that you *intend* to receive them.

And the action should be part of the fun. If the action isn't joyful, take another look at whether you really *want* this thing and whether you really *believe* you can have it.

For example, there was a man in one of my seminars who was lamenting that he had a speaking business but couldn't make any money. (That he was lamenting at all should be the first clue as to why he wasn't more successful.)

> Frank: *"Can you help me manifest some speaking gigs? I started speaking a year ago and I can't get jobs!"*

> Me: *"Frank, I know from my own experience in this industry that there are lots of clubs and associations that would love to hear you speak."*

> Frank: *"Yeah, I've called many of them but they all want me to speak for free."*

> Me: *"What's wrong with speaking for free? You could hone your skill, make contacts, and experience the joy of the work…"*

> Frank: *"Well, the thing is, I don't really like the speaking part. I like the money part. And speakers make a lot of money."*

Well, it is unlikely Frank is going to ever be one of those speakers. His thoughts, emotions and beliefs (flow of energy) were likely:

1. I don't have enough money (fear).
2. I can't do what I love and be well paid (hopelessness).
3. I must sacrifice my joy in order to prosper (martyr).
4. Money is hard to make (victim).
5. It's hard to be a successful speaker (self-pity).

His actions were neither joyful, nor were they bringing him closer to his desire. Are you beginning to see how these pieces of The Map fit together?

And note: I'm talking about taking *inspired* action. Not any old action for the sake of crossing it off the list.

WHAT IS INSPIRED ACTION?

Inspired action is action that feels good and right and fun. This inspiration to act generally comes *after you flow the energy.*

Have you ever had a wish or desire to do something that was a bit past your comfort zone? Have you ever talked yourself into thinking you could have it, become excited about the idea or concept and seen it fully manifest in your mind? From that place, taking action is fun—exciting even.

Have you also had a dream seem to fall apart in your mind before it even got started? From that place it is nearly impossible to act at all, let alone out of joy.

Why does this happen? Because the energy flow gets disrupted.

You begin to imagine the *failure*, not the *success* of the dream. And the desire to take action stops.

Inspiration to act comes *after* we feel like we are on the top of the world, like everything we desire is not only possible, but probable, like nothing can stop us.

Taking action ideally *strengthens* the dream and the flow. And then...

STEP FIVE: RESPONSE: HOW DOES YOUR REALITY RESPOND?

OK, you have a desire; you have fed it with positive energy and supported it by taking action. How do you know it's working?

Your reality will tell you if it is working! Is your reality changing? If so, how?

It doesn't take a long time to receive feedback. Your reality will often shift within hours. If you apply the techniques in this book, you will usually see a shift within a few days.

When I first began working on manifesting monetary abundance, I did a short (less than a minute) visualization technique. Two hours later I walked out to the mailbox and there was a check in the mail. The check was delivered to the wrong address, and it wasn't made out to me, but it was a check in *my* mailbox! *That was a sign that my desire was manifesting.*

Within a month the exact amount I desired (several thousand dollars) did come into my reality, but if I hadn't responded positively to the initial signs, it probably wouldn't have.

RESPONSE IN THIS SECTION OF THE MAP MEANS BOTH:

1. Look for the response in your world that your desires are manifesting *and*

2. How do you *respond to that response?*

In this case, I responded with excitement! My techniques were working!! I celebrated!

And what if you don't see your world changing, or, heaven forbid, your world changes in the opposite way—you have less money, etc.?

You respond accordingly...you go back to the dream, clarify it further, and go back to the flow and look for your hidden beliefs. I will show you how to do this later in this book.

STEP SIX: STAY IN THE PRESENT MOMENT AND IN JOY...AS IF YOU WERE LIVING THE DREAM.

In order to allow your dream to manifest elegantly, easily and without struggle, you have to keep those good vibes flowing. How?

By feeling as much joy as you can, staying in the present moment while living your life (emotionally) as if you already have what you desire!

This is a critical piece, folks. So many people spend five minutes hoping for their dreams and the next sixteen hours of their day focused on scarcity, struggle and lack.

You are flowing energy all day long. Be conscious of that and flow some love, joy and positivity.

And if you can think of yourself already having the dream, all the better! Your creation can manifest super fast!

How do you do that?

Here's one example: During the years I was learning about manifesting abundance I was driving an old, junky car. I imagined myself driving a new, jazzy convertible. I drove the old car as if it were the most expensive car in the world. I took care of it, kept it clean and treated it like it was worth one hundred times its value.

Guess what I currently drive? Not one but two beautiful red convertibles (one for each country!).

And that's all there is to conscious creation, folks...*unless*, you want it to be easier, more elegant and more fun. What then?

STEP SEVEN: ASK FOR HELP.

You *can* do it alone. But you don't have to. You have support from beyond this physical plane. You have unseen friends, such as God, Goddess, your higher self, your soul, your guides, your angels and more. Scores of them.

They want to help you but (remember the "free will universe" part?) *they won't interfere unless you ask*. So invite them in. And receive their help, their guidance, their support, their healing. They won't do it for you, but they will give you a leg up.

THESE ARE THE BONES OF THE MAP

However growth is not linear. Yes, this book is set out in a very linear fashion. And sometimes you will follow The Map as the book is written, straight through.

But more often, especially after you become proficient at conscious creation, you will move around The Map as if in a dance, focusing on what feels right in the moment. It can be a beautiful dance, rich and rewarding in ways even beyond your imagination.

However, The Map *does* give you a template to begin your process. And it works. It works. Isn't that awesome?!

MY JOURNEY AND THE MAP

When I first began to consciously create I didn't know what I was doing. At first I thought the best technique was having a lot of emotion and really, really, really wanting something. My techniques looked more like strained constipation than poised, graceful creating. Yet I somehow had some successes—in spite of myself!

But I had a lot of failures too. It was not a straight shot up. I had some deep disappointments. I had dreams shredded. But here, my stubbornness worked in my favor. I kept at it.

One of my first attempts at creating was to try to increase my income. Back then there was never enough money and I desperately wanted that to change.

Notice the word "desperate" in that sentence. Desperation is not the energy you want to flow when creating anything.

I did some techniques, and I had success; money came in quite magically. My husband was given an unexpected bonus at work! *"Hurray!"* I thought, *"My magic is working!"* I had the money spent before the check cleared.

Just three days later our car broke down and required exactly the same amount of money to repair. I had less money than before I'd started. I wanted to scream, *"What gives?!"*

If I'd had The Map back then, I might have realized that my world was responding (money coming in but the same amount leaving) to a belief (such as *"there is always just barely enough money"*). But I didn't; so I just became extremely frustrated and doggedly kept going.

There was no resource back then that laid out the steps and explained the reasoning quite as succinctly as The Map. But at the end of the day, when I finally figured it out, it was The Map I was following, however inelegantly.

My journey of creating the life I love was filled with stops and starts and if graphed out might look suspiciously like a roller coaster. At this stage, my creational journey is less a roller coaster than the graceful soaring of an eagle. There are still ups and downs but they are self-chosen. Sometimes I choose to slow down, rest and rejuvenate before venturing into the creational realm again.

The upside of all my mis-creating is *The Map*—a tool for *you* to use to avoid such steep descents. The Map won't take all the dips away. There are some valuable lessons you won't want to miss. But it *will* make it easier.

I'll bet you are becoming anxious to begin your own journey of manifestation. So where do *you* begin?

LIFE-ALTERING TAKE AWAYS

Read these slowly. Meditate on them or sit and contemplate them. Let them in. Let them change you.

+ There is a more *real* "you" who chose to come to this planet. That part of you wanted to experience certain things this lifetime. Before you were born you chose your parents, your siblings, the time and place of your birth and some of your childhood experiences. Obviously you also chose to forget just about everything you knew once you were born.

+ Time lag is the time it takes for something to manifest in time and space. A thought and feeling you had two weeks ago could manifest in your reality today. Time lag makes people believe what they see, instead of realizing they see what they believe (and think and feel).

+ Conscious creation is a whole new way of life for almost every one of us. It took decades to get to where we are with the old way of life. Learning a new one takes some time and effort. But again, the results are worth it.

YOUR NEXT STEPS

☐ Answer these questions in your journal:

- How important is creating the life of your dreams to you?

- How much effort are you willing to put forth to create it?

- What hesitations, fears and doubts do you have? Write about these, and release them. Simply say, *"I hereby release my hesitations, fears and doubts about creating a life I love."*

☐ In the space you have created, feel the excitement, the joy, the pure delight because you will (finally) be living the life of your dreams.

You are a part of everything. You create your own reality. You are a divine spark of consciousness – a part of God, a part of Goddess, a part of God, a part of Goddess, a part of everything.

THREE

WHO *ARE* YOU, REALLY?

"You are a spark of consciousness, a piece of the Divine. You are divine, by your very nature. You are a powerful light being and reality creator, here to do your personal and global work. You are loved by God/Goddess/All That Is and never forgotten. You are a being of infinite value and worth. You are worthy of all great things. Claim your divine reality creatorship. Own your Love, and radiate your Light to your world."

—GALEXIS

Most people live and die without realizing who they really are or why they came to this planet. This is not surprising, given that we all came here with the intent to forget who we are for the sole purpose of rediscovering ourselves.

You have been given a gift of the gods. You have the power and ability to create your world.

And why do you think you were given such a phenomenally amazing gift? Because you are worthless? Because you are hopeless? Flawed? Less than others? Lacking?

Of course not. You have been given this amazing gift because you are a God-being. You are by your very *nature*, divine. You are a piece of God and Goddess and you have been given a gift: the *ability to create*.

It is important for you to *own* this, to let it in and allow it to permeate your being. The more you own your own divinity, the easier and more elegantly you will be able to manifest the realties you desire.

This doesn't make you special, because everyone and everything is divine. It does, however, make you far more powerful than you have likely ever imagined. It also makes you *connected* to everyone and everything else in the multiverse.

WHAT MIGHT *STOP* YOU FROM OWNING YOUR DIVINITY?

Feeling regret about the past can stop you from letting in the true nature of your being.

Oh I understand, you haven't always *acted* like a God-being. Neither have I.

I have done and said things I regret. I have hurt others and myself. But I *know* the only way to move into the being I know I am, is to *let go* of those experiences.

How do you let go of things you wish you'd never done?

You forgive yourself.

You realize that despite being a spark of the Divine, you are also human. You have made mistakes and you will make more. It doesn't make you any less divine.

And if there is something you just cannot move beyond, find someone to help you through it. Self-judgment stemming from past regrets will not only stop you from recognizing your divinity, it will stop you from creating a life you love.

Another reason you might not let it in? If you feel you aren't yet worthy, or perfect enough, or deserving of such a designation.

If these thoughts and feelings come up for you, just make note of them. They may be a clue about a core belief, which we will cover in-depth in chapter six.

But for now, know that even if you don't feel it, you *are* worthy, deserving and perfect in your divinity. There is nothing you could do or say or be that could take that away or stop the Divine from loving you.

WHAT WILL STRENGTHEN THIS KNOWING?

Our world is set up for us to forget. But in order to create a delicious life we have to keep remembering *who* we are and *what* we are capable of.

You will need to be proactive in order not to forget. One way to accomplish this is to carve out time to just be with yourself. Call in your higher self, your guardian angel or your guides to sit with you, and allow them to love and help you in remembering and acknowledging who you are.

You can do this anytime and anywhere that you can be emotionally peaceful...while walking in nature, sitting quietly or in an actual meditation.

HOW I STRENGTHENED MY KNOWING

Getting to know my unseen friends has made a huge difference in owning my own divinity. After all, if my higher self is an aspect of me, and she is divine, then I must be also.

Early on, this concept seemed extremely foreign to me. I was shocked when my experiences in meditations began to prove just how *real* they are.

I remember when I began a relationship with one of my female guides. She said her name was Shaheba. In the first meditation with her, I noticed her bright blue eyes and strikingly warm hands—those hands were warmer than any I'd ever touched, in or out of meditation!

But then months went by before I met with her again. I had totally forgotten how warm her hands were. But in the next meditation I did with her, Shaheba took my hands in hers, and that intense, warm heat was there again.

"Oh my gosh," I thought, *"How could I have forgotten this?"*

And then I thought, *"Oh my God! If I had forgotten and her hands are* still *this warm, I'm not making this up! She is real!"*

And I'm not the only one with "real" unseen friends. *You* have a higher self. You have guides, and others who are available to assist you this lifetime. Feeling them close to you, whether in or out of meditation, is a good way to begin to know them. You don't need any special skill or ability. And you can have fun with it.

One time, as I was just getting to know my higher self, I asked her what her name was during a visualization. And I tried to guess…*"Is it Genevieve? Is it Mary? Is it Charlotte?"*

She looked at me, and said, *"If you won't stop talking how can you listen?"*

"Oh," I said, and became still.

And by gosh I heard it…*"It's Irahna,"* she told me. It was clear and solid, and I absolutely *knew* I did not make that up.

In the years since, I have established deep and loving relationships with Irahna and my guides, as well as many others. They *are* real. And the realness of those relationships has solidified my knowing of who *I* really am.

SOMETIMES YOUR UNSEEN FRIENDS WILL *HELP* YOU REMEMBER

When life becomes overwhelming, when things don't turn out as you'd hoped, when you slip back into old patterns and forget who you are, you will be reminded to stop and remember. You'll be reminded of what is real—through a dream, by a friend or a book, or simply by a thought.

When I first became attracted to metaphysics and spirituality, I was fascinated with the concept of reality creation but like most people, I had a life. And it was packed. I had two preschool children, I was working on a graduate degree and I maintained a home and a full social schedule. There would be long periods of time in which I would forget there was more to this world than meets the eye.

But my unseen friends would remind me. How?

My watch would stop.

Now this had a particular meaning for me. You see, one day I happened to see a TV talk show. The guest on the show was talking about the amazing powers of the mind and demonstrated this by flowing energy into stopped watches to get them working again.

I happened to have a watch with a dead battery that I had been meaning to take to the jeweler. I dug it out of the drawer and tried the exercise I saw on TV. It began ticking.

This was amazing to me. It spoke to me of all that is possible in this world that we are not aware of. To me, starting that watch was a symbol that *I* was more than I had known. And more was possible than I had imagined. It begged the question: *What else am I capable of?*

From then on, my unseen friends would stop my watch to remind me to wake up. No matter what watch I was wearing, or how new the battery was, "watch stopping" was the way they got my attention.

And it worked. I remembered. And I continued my search for truth.

They have reminded me in other ways too. One time a book fell from my bookshelf and landed in the middle of the room—five *feet* away from the bookshelf—and opened to a certain page. *That* got my attention.

You will receive messages and reminders too. Be open...to the guidance, the love and the assistance of your unseen friends. And when *you* are reminded or simply remember that there is more to you than meets the eye...give yourself that gift of reconnecting to yourself and to Source. Own again, who you are and what you came here to do.

It will strengthen your flow, it will raise your resonance, and it will make all of your creations easier and more elegant.

Because it *is* true. You are a piece of God, a piece of Goddess. And you are loved. Deeply, unequivocally, unconditionally loved.

TECHNIQUES TO DISCOVER MORE OF WHO YOU REALLY ARE:

PRE-SLEEP REQUEST TECHNIQUE

Before sleep, *say* this mentally or aloud: *"Higher self...please help me to see and own more of who I really am. Help me to remove whatever may be in the way of recognizing my divinity and the power and ability I have to create my reality. Please show me and guide me in gentle, loving and easy ways, with harm to none. Thank you, higher self."*

BLENDING WITH YOUR HIGHER SELF TECHNIQUE

Find a quiet place to sit or lie down where you will not be disturbed. Put on some soft music and get comfortable.

Before you close your eyes, say this mentally or aloud: *"Higher self...I would like you to join me in this blending. Please make your presence and your love known to me. I seek to have a greater knowing of who I really am, and to open to my divinity and my God-given ability to create my reality. Please help me with these intentions with gentleness, love, joy, grace and harm to none."*

Next gently close your eyes. And feel the presence of your higher self, enveloping you in love. Allow the love to heal you, support you and teach you. Open to the experience of knowing of who you really are.

You may sense your higher self as a light, or warmth or simply a loving presence. You may *see* your higher self in human form in your mind's eye, and they may come to lie or sit next to you. Or you may simply *feel* them being there.

You may think you are making it up and that's OK. Imagining them makes it easier to actually perceive them. The way they look may change during the blending or over subsequent blendings or meditations. Trust yourself.

Spend five or ten minutes with your higher self. And when you're finished, write down your experience. Let it be real.

YOUR NURTURING UNIVERSE TECHNIQUE

One of the ways the universe delivered my "best of everything" request was to offer me an opportunity to experience the amazing world beneath the sea. I became a certified scuba diver in Raja Ampat, Indonesia—the ultimate dive experience and, by some accounts, the last pristine dive location in the world.

Although I enjoyed diving, I must admit it freaked me out. Being dependent on a piece of equipment for your very life while one hundred feet beneath the sea was a bit daunting.

I began to look for reasons not to dive. And worse, I began to panic underwater. Panic is the one thing a diver should *never* do. Pretty much everything bad that can happen to a diver can be handled safely *if* you know what to do and have the presence of mind to do it.

At that point I realized *I* was doing this to me. I was a good diver. I had good equipment and great instruction. How could I look at this differently?

I began to see the ocean not as a threatening, dark and scary place, but as womb-like, nurturing, loving and sensual place. I began to see the ocean as the open arms of the Goddess— ready to receive me, love me, protect me and show me the beautiful gifts she had created.

Of course my experience changed dramatically. I felt drawn to the ocean, supported, protected and loved and I never panicked again.

With the following technique, I hope to shift your perception of *your* world in the same way I shifted my perception of the ocean.

Find a place to sit quietly. Put on some soft music and light a candle. Breathe deeply and exhale...allowing yourself to relax. Feel the air around you, wrapping you in a gentle embrace of love.

Imagine that air around you forming a bubble...a bubble of light and love extending two feet beyond your body. Everything that enters this bubble seeks to love you. Everything that enters this bubble seeks to support you.

This bubble is filled with nurturing love for you. It is the love of God, of Goddess. It is the love of the Divine seeking to connect with you and strengthen your knowing of their love for you. Now imagine the bubble expanding to the size of the room.

Then allow the bubble to expand to the size of your house. Imagine this entire house-sized bubble nurturing you, support-ing you, loving you. Now let the bubble grow...and grow...and grow...to the size of your neighborhood, the size of your city, your country. Let the bubble expand around the entire planet.

This is your world. *You* get to choose if it is threatening or loving. Choose loving. Imagine how your life would change, if the world were conspiring to say "yes" to your every dream. Imagine how it would feel to live in a world where everywhere you looked you were met with support, love, guidance and acceptance.

Sit for as long as you like, in what is becoming...*your world.*

Know that these techniques may be challenging at first. Owning your divinity is a process, and you will become better at it over time. Be patient. Self-discovery, as well as self-love, is a lifelong art.

LIFE-ALTERING TAKE AWAYS

Read these slowly. Meditate on them or sit and contemplate them. Let them in. Let them change you.

+ You are by your very *nature*, divine. You are a piece of God and Goddess and you have been given a gift: the *ability to create.*

+ Feeling regret about the past can stop you from letting in the true nature of your being. How do you let go of things you wish you'd never done? You *forgive* yourself. You realize that despite being a spark of the Divine, you are also human. You have made mistakes and you will make more. It doesn't make you any less divine.

+ Carve out some time to just be with yourself. Call in your higher self or your guides to sit with you, and allow them to love and help you in remembering and acknowledging who you are.

+ Be open...to the guidance, the love and the assistance of your unseen friends. It will strengthen your flow, it will raise your resonance, and it will make all of your creations easier and more elegant. Because it is true. You are a piece of God, a piece of Goddess. And you are loved. Deeply, unequivocally, unconditionally loved.

YOUR NEXT STEPS

☐ Sit with the knowing that you are a "God-being." Don't just say the words. *Feel it.* What if it is true? (It is.) You have been bestowed with this gift. Can you think of anything *more* insulting than to ignore it? Honor it, and yourself, by allowing time to contemplate it. Let it be real. Own who you (really) are.

☐ Say the **Pre-sleep Request** nightly for seven days. In your journal, write down any meaningful dreams or insights during this time period.

☐ Try the **Blending with Your Higher Self** technique or **Your Nurturing Universe** or both if time permits, at least once during the seven-day period.

Desire

You create your own reality. You are a divine spark of consciousness - a part of God, a part of Goddess, a part of everything.

FOUR

CLARIFYING YOUR DREAM

"If we aren't following a dream, then we
also don't know what we are walking towards,
and we don't help to make it happen."

—ANAIS NIN

I have known hundreds of very "spiritual" and/or "metaphysical" people, who *knew* they created their own reality, yet lived lives of scarcity, fear and lack. These people can recite the elements of conscious creation verbatim, but can't create themselves out of a paper bag.

Why?

It's one thing to know theory. It's another thing altogether to *apply* the theory. *Conscious creation is a lot of work.*

Don't get me wrong. It gets easier. But even after you've proven to yourself that you *know* the steps and can *change* your reality, it is *still* a lot of work. There is never a day when you can say, *"OK, I created a great life now; I can forget about how I got here and just enjoy it."*

Every day requires staying conscious and putting forth the flow to maintain what you've created. Every new dream requires following The Map all over again.

Is it worth it? Heck yeah! Your life can be heaven on earth...of course it is worth it.

But you have to be willing to put in the effort. And where does your luscious life begin?

It begins with a dream. And where do you begin to build a dream?

DREAMS BEGIN WITH INTENTIONS

There are lots of ways to begin to dream. I've known people to work with dream boards, goal setting and magic boxes. And while none of these are wrong, and I might very well use them at some point, I am convinced that the most effective and elegant way to *begin* a dream is with *intentions*.

Intentions are statements of, well, intent. Intent is strong, clear and *willed*. And although we *are* talking about a dream or desire, the choice to turn that dream into an intention adds strength and commitment.

I looked to the dictionary to explain further:

> *Desire: A strong feeling of wanting to have something or wishing for something to happen.*

> *Intent: Resolve or determination to do something.*

Stating an intention moves the desire from a *wish* to a *commitment to create.*

Intentions aren't wishy-washy. They mean business. Intentions tell your conscious and subconscious minds, *"One way or another, I will create what I want."*

WHAT IF YOU DON'T KNOW
WHAT YOU WANT?

Inevitably someone says, *"I would love to create a life I love, but I have no idea what that is!"*

Well, with The Map, you don't *have* to know exactly what you want. You only have to know how you want to *feel*. And let's face it; everyone knows that they ultimately want to feel *good*.

So take one category at a time and add positive emotions, and voila! You have an intention.

For example, take the category of money. Even though you may not know how the money will come, or even how much money is "enough," you do know that you want enough money for everything you want. So begin by stating a broad, overall intention.

> *I intend to create enough money for all my needs and desires.*

Then add the emotions you want to feel after you receive the money:

> *I intend to create enough money for all my needs and desires. I intend that this money will make me feel abundant, secure, safe and financially free.*

And then you may want to expand it a bit.

> *I intend to create more than enough money for all my needs and desires. I intend that this money will make me feel abundant, secure, safe and financially free. I intend that this money will come to me in easy and elegant ways, with harm to none.*

And my friends, if you can't even get *that* far, begin with intending to discover your dream.

> *I intend to discover what I truly desire.*
> *I intend to discover which path and/or work would bring me the highest joy.*
> *I intend to discover the gift I came here to bring.*
> *I intend to discover the life I would love to live.*

WHAT IF YOU ONLY KNOW WHAT YOU *DON'T* WANT?

Sometimes knowing what you *don't* want can help you to figure out what you *do* want. Let's say some things have been going *wrong* in your life. Maybe...

> You find yourself divorced after sixteen years of marriage.
> Your house is being foreclosed upon.
> You are between jobs and have no idea where you will

find enough money to put food on the table, let alone gas in the car.

Your children moved in with your ex, and he then moves them across the country without telling you.

Your only living parent dies.

You give up your beloved pets because the only apartment that you could find without a credit check refuses pets.

Bills are accruing at such an alarming rate you fear you'll have to file for bankruptcy, and you do.

You are desperately trying to work a multi-level marketing company—putting every penny you have into leads and eking out a sale here and there only to have the new clients renege, forcing you to return the money.

Yes...this was my life in the late 90s. All of this happened within a year. I had no clue what a "life I loved" would look like, and now, looking back, there is no way I could have pictured the life I currently have. I couldn't have imagined a life this fabulous back then!

What I *did* know, was what I *didn't* want!

I didn't want to struggle.

I didn't want to be afraid I'd end up living in my car.

I didn't want to cry myself to sleep at night because I missed my children.

I didn't want to cringe in fear that a bill collector was

calling every time the phone rang.

I didn't want to be in a relationship with someone who wasn't committed to growing the relationship and who couldn't respect me.

I didn't want to be confused and uncertain about what I wanted or how to get there!

What would I say to the "me" who was in such a state?

I would say, *"First, forgive yourself for the reality you allowed to manifest."*

If you're having problems, before you do anything...forgive yourself. You can't create a *new* dream if you are still focusing energy on the *old* one, and lamenting the past is feeding the struggle.

Then begin where you are right *now*.

If you are clear about what you *don't* want, ask yourself, what *do* you want? My intentions might have looked like this:

I intend to create a life filled with ease and elegance.

I intend to create a life filled with safety, security and abundance.

I intend to unconditionally love my children, no matter what path they choose.

I intend to create a committed relationship in which I feel valued, respected and loved.

I intend to be clear, conscious and awake regarding my life direction.

I ask for guidance, support and assistance from my unseen friends including God and Goddess to manifest these or even greater intentions, with harm to none.

Note the addition of "with harm to none." When you are new to this work I suggest adding this phrase to protect yourself against any hidden beliefs you may have. You may hold beliefs you don't even know about, such as:

I must earn every penny I make, or

I am unworthy, or

It is wrong to make a lot of money and if I do I will be punished.

These types of beliefs could manifest as an accident with an insurance payout. You could have all the money you want but not be able to enjoy it. Yes, we did specify in "easy, elegant and fun ways," but this is powerful stuff and I like to err on the side of caution.

Eventually you will ferret out your sabotaging beliefs and change them and it won't be as important to add *"with harm to none."* But in the beginning, it is.

START WHERE YOU ARE

Whatever it is you *do* know, begin there. You can always revise them as you go along. Stating your desires in the form of an intention is something you may be doing for the rest of your life, once you begin to see the changes that come as a result. Your intentions will change and grow as you and your dreams change and grow.

Once you have written them you will read them often, and change them or add to them occasionally, but your core intentions will be done. But nothing is in stone. When you change your mind, simply change your intentions. I keep mine on my computer so changing and adding to them is super easy.

You can't do this wrong...you can only become more clear about what it is you truly desire.

So, where do you begin?

YOU BEGIN WITH YOUR "OVERALL" INTENTION

Your overall intention is the backbone of all your intentions. This is the broad stroke of how you want your life to be.

I highly recommend that your overall intention be written as an experiential or feeling state. This is not the place to get specific, but rather to set the stage for how the rest of the intentions will manifest for you.

Begin with where you are today. How wonderful and elegant can you imagine your life becoming? Then, allow your overall intention to develop and change as *you* grow and change.

Here is one example of an overall intention:

> *I intend to live the life I was born to live; and as fully and as elegantly as possible, discover my genius, live a life I love, and consciously create my reality with fun, joy and laughter.*

NEXT WRITE YOUR "CORE" INTENTIONS

Core intentions address every category of your life. They are broad strokes, yes, but focused on a certain area of your life. Core intentions are where most of your intentions will be.

Core intention categories might include:

> Loving partnership intentions
> Other relationship intentions (such as children, friends, parents, co-workers, etc.)
> Work intentions
> Physical body intentions
> Spiritual intentions
> Physical environment intentions
> Mental and emotional intentions
> Play intentions
> Creative intentions
> Financial intentions
> Earth and humanity intentions
> Cosmic intentions

CORE INTENTIONS SHOULD BE AS UNSPECIFIC (AS TO HOW IT LOOKS) AS POSSIBLE

I've seen many people shoot themselves in the foot by thinking they know more than the universe as to how something should manifest. There are literally *millions* of possibilities as to how something such as abundance, success or love could manifest in the world, and yet most people seem to limit themselves to one or two!

Here is an example of a *specific* core intention regarding career:

I intend to receive a promotion to manager of my department before the end of the year.

That intention is saying, "*I know more than the universe about the best possible scenario for me.*"

What if the company goes belly up in November?

What if a new company moves to town and they have an opening you're perfect for, not as a manager but as a vice president?

What if a person were to come into your life in January who wanted to start a company with you—an experience that would fill your heart with joy and your pocketbook with money?

You cannot know the best possible scenario. So don't even try. It's far more fun and exponentially more rewarding to let the universe handle the details.

Here is a rewrite of the previous intention that is *unspecific* (as to how it looks), and a thousand times more powerful as to how it can manifest:

I intend to create work that is rewarding and excit-ing, pays more than I can even imagine, has fun and creative co-workers and is ideally located. I intend that this job will make me feel prosperous, joyous, creative, appreciated, respected, excited and eternally thankful!

Notice that this intention does not rule out the possibility that your current job could provide the rewards you are seeking. Your current job could shift and provide you with everything described in the intention. But if it can't, the intention will open the door for you to manifest other possibilities.

Let's take a look at a *specific* (as to how it looks) intention around money:

I intend to receive a ten percent raise this year at review time.

This intention says, "OK, *universe, even though there may be more than a million possible ways for me to manifest money, I have decided that it must come through my current job. And even though money is an illusion and I can have as much illusion as I want, I want exactly and only ten percent more money.*"

Why limit yourself that way? This intention holds too tightly to the form, which will slow down the flow of energy considerably. This will make it much more difficult and time consuming to manifest.

You also haven't specified anything but the money and where it must come from.

What if your boss leaves and you can't stand the new one?

What if the company moves to a place you don't want to live?

What if the company starts to do poorly, they let people go and you have to take on another employee's job—in addition to your own—for the same pay?

It's much more powerful to state a money intention like this:

> *I intend to create more than enough money in easy, elegant and fun ways, and for this abundance to fill me with safety, security, freedom and ease. I intend for this money to manifest in perfect timing with harm to none.*

STATING YOUR DREAMS AS NON-SPECIFIC INTENTIONS

Transforming your dreams and desires into non-specific intentions is more of an art than a skill. You will become better at this when you realize how powerful it is to let the universe handle the specifics.

Basically you simply think about how you will *feel* once you *have* the thing you want. And then you think about the various aspects of this dream, and how you will feel when you manifest all the details of this thing you want, without specifying what it will look like.

Say, for instance, you want a job you enjoy that pays well.

This is what your intention might be:

> *I intend to create a job I love that makes me feel excited, creative, prosperous, abundant, joyful and appreciated.*

You might also add:

> *I intend that this job will be filled with fun, positive challenges, and co-workers I love to work with.*

Also add an intention about compensation:

> *I intend to be well compensated for this job, with a salary that is more than I had expected. And I intend that this job will have ample opportunities for advancement and ongoing education.*

And don't forget about logistics:

> *I intend that this job I love will be in a place I love, with hours, workdays and a location that fits my temperament perfectly.*

You may even add an intention about the physical atmosphere:

I intend that this job will be in a beautiful setting, with an office that is bright, healthy, clean, vibrant and creative.

Doesn't that sound like fun? Doesn't it get you excited to think that you could create such a job? If it seems too good to be true, you probably have a belief about how good life can get for you or that you don't deserve something so spectacular. Jot it down. You will discover how to change these beliefs in chapter six.

Let's look at an example of non-specific (as to how it looks) intentions around a loving partnership:

I intend to create a deeply loving relationship with a (wo)man. I intend that this relationship will bring us love, fun, safety, security, laughter, freedom, trust, respect, intimacy and joy.

Next, you might think about what makes a successful partnership. You might come up with some items such as similar values, beliefs and priorities. Write an intention that includes them such as:

I intend that my partner shares compatible core and spiritual ideals, values, beliefs and priorities in life and that he/she has the character and integrity to live by those ideals, priorities and values.

You might remember relationships from your past that disappointed you in one way or another. Write some intentions to address any past concerns, such as:

I intend that the (wo)man in my loving partnership is emotionally and physically available.

I intend that the (wo)man in my loving partnership is emotionally mature and of sound mind and body.

I intend that the (wo)man in my loving partnership is as committed to creating a caring, loving and growing partnership as I am.

And don't forget lifestyle issues:

I intend that we share compatible ideas of lifestyle, including how to keep and decorate a home, divide chores and spend our free time.

Physical compatibility:

I intend that my loving partner and I are beautifully compatible physically—including our sexual preferences, the amount of energy we have, our sleep patterns, our eating habits and the way we spend our physical time together.

And money:

> *I intend that we come to easy agreements about how we share, bring in, save and spend our money.*

Perhaps children are or will be in the picture:

> *I intend that we are in agreement on whether to have children and how many children to have. I intend that we are in agreement on overall parenting principles and that we balance and support each other well in our parenting roles.*

Don't forget to create compatibility with your families and friends:

> *I intend that my loving partner and I enjoy spending time with each other's family and friends—adding to each other's joy and fulfillment in life; and that we share similar concepts about being in and responding to these relationships.*

Now that you have created your perfect partner, add your ideal location:

> *I intend to create this loving relationship in a physical area I love that is easy, fun, healthy and joyful for me to reside in.*

Of course if you leave something out and the universe delivers *almost* the whole package, no worries. Just revise your intentions. Contrary to popular belief, opportunity knocks more than once. In fact it knocks as many times as you believe it knocks!

WRITING YOUR "IMMEDIATE" INTENTIONS

Your immediate intentions are the intentions for the projects and creations that are your top priority right now. This is where it is appropriate (but not necessary) to be more specific.

For example, if one of your core intentions is:

> *I intend to create more than enough money with ease, elegance, freedom and joy.*

And you had an interview coming up for a job you would love that would pay well, an immediate intention may be:

> *I intend to be offered a job with _____ company (or another company even better than that) for great pay and wonderful benefits as soon as possible.*

Notice the intention still leaves the door open for an even better company or offer.

Or, an immediate intention may touch on a current event or holiday:

> *I intend to allow the holidays to be conscious, joyful and easy. I intend to let go of all preconceived notions and expectations of "how it should be" and open to the possibility that the best holiday may be entirely different then what I've experienced before.*

Or an immediate intention could cover an upcoming gathering with people who are not the easiest to be around:

> *I intend that my mother's birthday party will be enjoyable, loving, easy and fun for me to attend.*

Or an immediate intention may be around a home you want to buy:

> *I intend to buy the home located at _____ (or a home even more wonderful than that) for a great price with terms that I love, in the perfect timing.*

Your immediate intentions are the ones you will use the rest of The Map to manifest. While your core intentions are always manifesting in the background if you give them at least a little energy, your immediate intentions are the ones you will make your top priority.

Immediate intentions will change often. Sometimes you will

move a core intention to an immediate intention and vice versa.

And lastly,

WRITE YOUR "CLOSING INTENTION AND REQUEST"

This is a "bonus" section if you really want to kick your intentions into gear. This is where you turn to your unseen friends and ask for their energy, light and love.

It's also where you open to the possibility that your unseen friends may have something even *better* in mind.

Each and every time I write or speak my intentions I close with this statement:

> ***Request to my unseen friends:*** *I request and intend to receive help from all of my unseen friends to manifest all of my intentions even greater than stated, with harm to none.*

Intentions

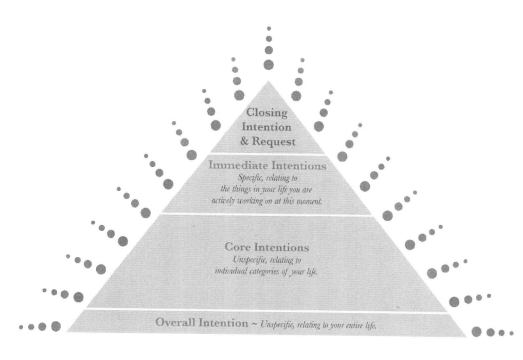

Closing
Intention
& Request

Immediate Intentions
*Specific, relating to
the things in your life you are
actively working on at this moment.*

Core Intentions
*Unspecific, relating to
individual categories of your life.*

Overall Intention ~ *Unspecific, relating to your entire life.*

SOME TIPS ON WRITING INTENTIONS

Be clear: Be sure your intentions are worded as concisely and cleanly as possible. Your subconscious mind should not be confused as to what you *really* want. Instead of this:

> *I intend to figure out what I want to do with my life. I love basketball and fishing and my fiancée, Kirsten. (I need to be successful not just for myself and my happiness but I want to make her happy as well.) I wouldn't*

mind running my own business but I'm not sure where to start let alone what avenue to go down. Oh, how can I associate what I love into making wealth and health, and it would be happiness by default?

Try something like this:

I intend to become clear and decisive around a career path that I love.

I intend that this career is enjoyable and exciting, that it fits my temperament, gifts, talents and skills, and that it pays well and manifests in perfect timing with harm to none.

Be excited: It is also important to have some excitement around your intentions. If you are not excited about the possibility of creating these things, why even include them in the first place? Emotion creates. Instead of this:

I intend to create a relationship.

Try something like this:

I intend to create a life partner that I absolutely love to be with! This relationship will fill me with joy, safety, trust, love, excitement, passion, intimacy and security. I intend to feel fully and unconditionally loved in this relationship. I intend that this person will come into my life easily, elegantly, in perfect timing and with harm to none.

Be tangible: Don't include only intentions for non-tangible things such as emotional well being. Intend to have *things* you can measure, so you can tell if you are succeeding. Money, jobs, friends, partners, children, homes and cars are all perfectly fine things to create.

Some people tell me they have no need for things, money, etc. They say their lives are perfect and they just want to manifest happiness. I say that's a cop-out. People who say this are either afraid to dream (if it fails, there goes their "perfection") or don't feel they deserve to dream.

Sure, eventually you won't need more money or houses, but there will still be tangible things to dream into your life. I recently created a lovely new friendship. And although I don't have need for more money per se, the success of this work is also a dream of mine, and very tangible.

And if you really don't have another tangible thing you want (you must be really good at this already)...certainly you can dream some tangible things for the world?

Be believable: Although you *do* want to create things you don't currently have, they should also be within the realm of possibility. Of course anything is possible, but you might not believe that yet.

If you want to create winning the lottery but are currently living on welfare in your sister's basement, that's not a dream, it's a fantasy.

If you want to become a brain surgeon but you barely made it through high school and you're ninety-five years old, it's not likely to happen.

Your dreams should be a stretch, but not so much of a stretch that they are beyond your current reach. How can you tell if you are not dreaming true dreams, but fantasizing unrealistic ones?

Ask yourself, do I really *expect* this to happen? And be totally honest with the answer.

If you are just a bit shaky in your expectation, no problem. The remaining steps in The Map will handle that. But if you are using a fantasy as a way to escape reality, beware. It won't serve you if you *really* want to learn how to do this.

However, sometimes a dream is just too big for *now*, and needs to be broken down into baby steps. The jobless dreamer who wants to win the lottery might be better off to first dream a job that allows him a place of his own. He can *then* expand that dream to create more and more prosperity as his beliefs and self-concept expand.

Be positive: Don't use words like "*don't,*" "*not,*" or "*except*" in your intentions. Such as,

> *I intend to create a loving relationship with a person who is not selfish.*

Your mind will not hear the "*not,*" and link "*relationship*" and "*selfish.*" Guess what you will create? It will be much more effective to state it this way:

> *I intend to create a loving relationship with a person who is graciously generous.*

Be (brutally) honest: This is your *life* we are talking about, folks. Your life in which *anything* you dream can come true. Why waste this power and ability on dreams that are not true to your heart?

Take some time to contemplate what your *real* dreams are. And let old and worn dreams die. How do you know the difference?

Begin by asking yourself *why* you want any given dream. If the answer has anything to do with *proving* to others, or *showing* others, or being *better than* others or *as good as* others...let it go. It isn't your dream. It is your ego's dream, or your parent's dream, or someone else's dream.

Then think about having the dream. It should excite you! It should feel joyous and fun.

If you are uncertain as to how you will feel when you have it, see if you can somehow test it out. If there is a state or country you dream of living in, plan a visit or vacation there. If there is an industry you dream of working in, see if you can arrange an internship. Try out your dreams in any way you can.

Sometimes we hold onto the dreams of our youth because it is a fun fantasy. Evaluating all of your dreams from the perspective of your adult self may save you energy, time and money down the road.

One of my dreams as a girl was to own a horse. I loved horses and I continued to hold the dream of owning my own horse well into my adult years. In my late forties, I met the man who would become my husband, and he owned three horses! I could ride anytime I wanted. My dream had come true!

I rode the horses a handful of times. Brushing and saddling them was a lot of work, and not nearly as much fun as I'd imagined. My dream of owning a horse was my adolescent's dream. Not mine. That was a dream I should have let die.

If your dreams are truly the dreams of "you the adult" and the very idea of them coming true really excites you, you are on the right track.

Be willing to keep them up: You will never be finished with your intentions because you will never be finished dreaming new dreams. Remember intentions work best when you continue to revisit them, revise them and expand them.

HOW I WORK WITH INTENTIONS

I work with intentions regularly. I read them, add to them and rewrite them as needed. I pay particular intention to the *immediate* intentions. I change these often, because my life is changing often. I rank that list, putting the most important intentions at the top of the list. I delete those that have manifested and add those to my "success" journal. And I move those I'm not that focused on at the moment back to core intentions.

I also rewrite the core intentions as I'm moved to. When I read them, I expect them to move me emotionally. If they don't, I strengthen them until they do. They should also reflect *everything* I desire. So, for example, today I read the intentions for this book, and this one stood out:

> *I intend for this book to serve as a map to help people learn the principles of conscious creation. I intend for this book to help people to successfully create their own realities, reduce their fear and increase their esteem, power and love.*

I felt something was missing. The statement, which prior to today had been enough, needed to shift. I added the words "joy" and "success" at the end and for now, it is complete:

I intend for this book to serve as a map to help people learn the principles of conscious creation. I intend for this book to help people successfully create their own realities, reduce their fear and increase their esteem, power, love, joy and success.

To me, intentions serve as an overall blueprint for the life I want to live, and they also cover the specific things I want to manifest as well. Working regularly with my intentions is powerful as a focusing technique, but beyond that it serves me in three critically important ways:

1. **I strengthen my knowing of who I really am.** Every time I cross something off my list because it has manifested, I realize at a deeper and deeper level that I am a powerful reality creator.

2. **I remember all over again how this universe works.** It is easy for me to get sidetracked by all that is happening in my world and to forget that everything "out there" is generated by what is happening "inside" of me. As I work with my intentions and watch as they manifest over time, I am reminded of just how responsive our universe really is.

3. **I give my life the attention it deserves.** Most people spend more time planning their vacations than planning (or trying to manifest) their dreams. I don't

want to be one of those people. I want to live a life I love. My intentions are the basis of that creation.

Intentions are a wonderful way to become clear on what I want, and by the very act of writing them, I feel shifts and changes in who I am—and who I am becoming. *"If you do nothing else,"* I tell my friends, *"write your intentions."*

HOLDING INTENTIONS (NO MATTER WHAT HAPPENS)

It's hard for me to remember that I was *ever* financially challenged, but I was...big time. Not so many years ago I was jobless, my home was in foreclosure and I was nearly broke. Yes, I "got happy" and that stopped the downward spiral. But you still have to do the pro-active creation work to make something great happen in your world.

I held an intention to create a job that allowed me to meet my bills so that I could focus on starting my own company. I flowed energy towards this intention and took action by working as a temp one day a week. Sure enough within a couple of weeks I was offered a job in the marketing department of a large mortgage company!

The bad news was the location—the office was at the other end of town and I would have to commute over an hour each way. I gulped, and turned down the job. It just was too long a schlep especially since I wanted to focus time and energy on the dream of my own company.

I kept up the flow though. That night I did some techniques to manifest a job I loved, with good pay and a reasonable commute that would pay the bills until I could open my own company.

The very next day, I was offered the job again, but with the ability to work from home four days a week *and* flexible hours on the one day I had to drive to the office!

I told my boss-to-be that I would be leaving at some point to begin my own venture and promised to give her ample notice. I had a blast at this place and honed lots of skills I didn't even know I had!

I practiced feeling as though I had my dream job at the helm of my own company, even when things got stressful at work. Sometimes I would steal away into the bathroom, leaving the deadlines, chaos and frenetic people behind.

I'd close my eyes and feel the way I *wanted* to feel at work... peaceful, powerful, creative, successful, abundant, joyful and excited. I was able to go back to work feeling that way and with practice I was able to hold the feelings for longer and longer periods of time.

One year later, I was given another opportunity with the president of this multi-billion dollar corporation. He was leaving the mortgage company and starting two new ventures—both a mortgage and a marketing company! He offered the entire marketing staff a job and me a piece of the company!

My dream was coming true! Although the piece was miniscule and I wouldn't be vested for years, I owned (at least part of) a company! I immediately quit and went to work for him.

As vice president of a start-up, I worked nonstop and discovered even more of what I could do. Again, I had a heck of a good time, but it didn't last. In six months, the company closed. And again I was jobless.

Was my magic not working? Should I change something? What was going on?

I eventually calmed down and went back to what I know… that flowing energy to my intention will manifest it. Period. I made the decision to view this experience as a blessing in disguise. The loss of this dream would lead to something even *more* fun, rewarding and spectacular. I did techniques and imagined myself deliriously happy with my job. I practiced patience…an important skill but difficult to master when you have no job and no prospects of one.

Within a few weeks I was presented with an idea from the woman who was president of the start-up. She suggested that she and I take the remnants of the old company and begin our own. We each put in fifty dollars for the incorporation (which I did myself). And suddenly I found myself owning fifty percent of a company! Wow! My dream really *was* coming true!!

However, fifty percent of zero income is still zero. I knew the universe would support me in this transition; I kept up the flow and asked everyone I knew about part-time jobs. My new partner found two part time jobs for me that would pay the bills as I put as much time as possible into the new company.

I admit that sometimes my conviction waivered. I wondered, *was I moving forward, or backward*? But I did the only thing I knew would work: I held the intention and continued to flow energy to a life of abundance and a job I loved.

More bad news six months later…although the company was doing well enough for me to take a small salary, my partner was upset with me because, as the silent partner, she wasn't in control. *"This company isn't big enough for the both of us,"* she wrote me in an email, and suggested that I buy her out.

The problem was I had nothing to buy her out *with*. This was a fundamental problem that masked my bigger fear: *Could I do this on my own?* It was my partner who had years of real estate and marketing experience, not me. At that point, I had only a few years of experience in this field.

I looked at my beliefs yet again. I could change the one that said, *"I am not ready to run this company by myself"*. I did change that belief and a few others. I did more techniques to flow the energy. And I took the leap of faith and borrowed the money from a friend. I bought my partner out, became the full owner, and the company skyrocketed. My dream had come true despite the twists and turns that made me doubt myself...but not for long.

All those twists and turns had given me the knowledge, experience and skills (not to mention the confidence) to succeed at running my own company. I didn't know it at the time, but each step brought me closer to my dream—even that initial gig as a temp.

Without tangible proof, it's hard to trust that your dreams are manifesting. But it's your day-to-day, moment-to-moment thoughts and feelings that create your tomorrows. If you stay clear and focused no matter what happens (and The Map will help)...you can't *help* but create the life you love.

REALITY CHECK

I'm thrilled you are reading this book. Really. But reading this book will not create the life you love. Only following The Map will do that, and then only if you follow it genuinely.

If you are serious about living a life that is perfect for you, take a break now. Write out or beef up your intentions. Doing this work is the only thing that will change your reality. Remember, you don't have to be perfect, you just have to begin.

Need more examples?

SAMPLE INTENTIONS

OVERALL INTENTION:

I intend to experience greater and greater levels of magic, fun, creativity, connectedness with the Divine, peace, prosperity, abundance, safety, elegance, ease, health and healing, divine grace, divine guidance, joy, freedom, beauty, trust, wisdom and love.

IMMEDIATE INTENTIONS:

I intend to live every waking minute of every day conscious, awake and aware in the present moment, while feeling as much joy as possible.
I intend that all my rental properties move into a positive cash flow quickly, magically, easily and joyfully.
I intend to live the most beautiful life possible, with harm to none and benefit to all.
I intend to allow my companies to grow easily, elegantly and with a great deal of joy and love, into inspiring, healing, love-filled, fun and phenomenally successful corporations.

I intend to create the most loving relationship possible with my partner.

I intend to support my children in separate but loving ways without enabling, and to see them as the strong, loving, capable, creative and successful people they are.

I intend to change and/or transmute all subconscious and unconscious beliefs, drives, patterns and projections that keep me from living the life I was born to live.

I intend to refinance my home at the best rate possible.

I intend to have a blast at my in-laws' party next Saturday.

RELATIONSHIP INTENTIONS:

I intend to joyfully deepen my loving relationship with my partner, providing greater and greater levels of peace, safety, fun, freedom, ease, joy, intimacy, vulnerability, trust, play, creativity, expansion, positive activation, tenderness and love for us both.

I intend to open my heart, as fully as possible, to feel my partner's magnificent love.

I intend that my partner and I lovingly support each other in our individual dreams and goals.

I intend that my partner and I both feel deeply and richly loved and supported by the other.

I intend that my partner and I enjoy each other's lives, friends, families, children, interests and passions, while allowing freedom for each of us to enjoy our independent lives as well—enriching ourselves and each other through these experiences.

I intend that the communication between my partner and I be crystal clear, both with words and beyond words.

I intend to enjoy my relationship with my partner, allowing it to unfold and deepen with elegance and ease.

I intend that my partner and I find easy compromises and meet each other's needs while honoring our own. I intend that this will result in ideas and realities far better than either of us could originally conceive or create.

I intend, no matter what challenges or opportunities my partner and I face, to always remember the love.

OTHER RELATIONSHIP INTENTIONS:

I intend to deepen the loving, joyful and fulfilling relationship I have with each of my children.

I intend to positively support my children in living their lives with as much ease, elegance and joy as possible.

I intend to build loving relationships with as many of my partner's family and friends as possible.

I intend to develop friends with whom I'm emotionally, spiritually, mentally, physically and cosmically compatible.

I intend to create friends my partner and I both love to be with.

I intend to create conscious, loving, interactive and supportive relationships with my unseen friends, including, but not limited to my angels, higher self, soul and guides.

I intend that all of my relationships—esoteric, family, work-related, community-based, acquaintance or just in passing, be filled with as much fun, joy, love, light, kindness and compassion as possible.

I intend to lift those I connect with, however significantly or insignificantly, to greater levels of healing and loving. I intend to help them to recognize who they really are.

WORK INTENTIONS:

I intend every minute I work to be filled with fun, creativity, excitement, abundance, prosperity, joy, service and positive surprises.

I intend to create supportive, healthy and nurturing surroundings at work.

I intend to work with like-minded people who I enjoy immensely and feel greatly supported by.

I intend to find meaning in my work, be it the broadest dreams or tiniest details.

I intend to remember that I am sending positive energy to the greater whole whenever I am in joy.

I intend to gratefully and gracefully perform my

destiny work on this planet, in the perfect timing, with joy and fun, and with the highest level of positive impact possible.

PHYSICAL BODY INTENTIONS:

I intend that my physical body is one hundred percent vital, healthy and filled with energy.
I intend to keep my body weight at the range of _____ with ease and elegance.
I intend to reverse the aging process and fully rejuvenate my physical body. I intend to look and feel ageless.
I intend to be drawn to and crave the movement, food/supplements and body/energetic work that my body needs to stay in perfect shape. I intend that this will have the greatest positive impact on my physical, energetic, spiritual and mental bodies.

SPIRITUAL INTENTIONS:

I intend to strengthen my connection with the archangels and others from the angelic realm.
I intend to form a deeper and stronger bond on all levels with my unseen friends who support me in this lifetime.
I intend to deepen and strengthen my loving relationship with God and Goddess.

I intend to see, own and become who I really am as fully as possible.

PHYSICAL SURROUNDINGS INTENTIONS:

I intend to create home(s) that fill my family and me with peace, joy, happiness and safety, with elegance and ease.

I intend to elegantly and easily fill our surroundings with comfort, beauty, sensuousness and love, energetically and physically.

I intend that my home(s) are loving and transformative places for us and the people in our lives to grow, love and heal.

MENTAL AND EMOTIONAL INTENTIONS:

I intend to be a courageous adventurer and risk taker—secure and confident about who I am.

I intend to see beauty in everyone and everything I see.

I intend to feel totally safe and secure.

I intend to feel that I'm always in the right place at the right time for all of my intentions to come true.

I intend to live in the now and feel greater and greater depths of love, fun, joy, happiness, ecstasy, compassion and caring for myself and others.

I intend to have fun continuously, and to open (more

every day) to my creativity, psychic abilities and passion.

INTENTIONS FOR PLAY:

I intend to explore this delicious physical world, allowing my reality to guide me to experiences and adventures, information and knowing, and people who will delight me in every way.

CREATIVE INTENTIONS:

I intend to open fully and completely to the greatest depths of creativity possible. I intend to allow myself to express that creativity in a myriad of fun and enjoyable ways that include, but are not limited to, decorating, art and writing.

FINANCIAL INTENTIONS:

I intend unlimited cash and resources to flow into my life easily, abundantly and endlessly.
I intend my financial abundance to provide greater and greater levels of security, freedom, ease and elegance.
I intend to be guided to the institutions, individuals and projects that can be truly aided by my financial

and energetic contributions and to know deeply and surely when and what to support.

INTENTIONS FOR THE EARTH AND HUMANITY:

I intend to create a world filled with love, compassion and light with as much ease and elegance as possible.
I intend to aid the earth in her healing as much as I am capable.
I intend for those without a voice (people, animals, the earth, etc.) to be held in arms of love and light and for them to feel that love as much as possible.

COSMIC INTENTIONS:

I intend to work with my team of unseen friends and star families to aid in the recognition of the oneness of all that is.
I intend to work in union with God and Goddess to increase the love and support felt by and extended to "All That Is" in whatever way and to the highest extent that I am capable.
I intend to aid the multiverse in her healing as much as I am capable.
I intend to create a multiverse filled with love, compassion and light with as much ease and elegance as possible.

REQUEST TO MY UNSEEN FRIENDS:

I request and intend to receive help from all of my unseen friends to manifest all of my intentions even greater than stated, with harm to none.

OK. I WROTE MY INTENTIONS— NOW WHAT?

Read them—twice daily. Read them once in the morning and once before bed (at the very least read your overall and immediate intentions).

Change them whenever you feel they don't fully reflect what you desire. Be inspired and excited by them.

And focus energy on them (you will learn how to do this in the next chapter).

Desire is only the second step of The Map, remember? I never said it was easy, only that it was worth it.

LIFE-ALTERING TAKE AWAYS

Read these slowly. Meditate on them or sit and contemplate them. Let them in. Let them change you.

+ Every day requires staying conscious and putting forth the flow to maintain what you've created. Every *new* dream requires following The Map all over again.

+ Intent is strong, clear and *willed*. And although we *are* talking about a dream or desire, the choice to turn that dream into an intention adds strength and commitment. Stating an intention moves the desire from a *wish* to a *commitment to create*.

+ You don't have to know what you *want* to create a life you love. You only have to know how you want to *feel*. And let's face it; everyone knows that they ultimately want to feel *good*.

YOUR NEXT STEPS

☐ Spend some time contemplating your dream life. Are there any dreams you need to let die? If so, write them out, and let them go. Burn your list in a safe place (such as over the kitchen sink).

☐ Write your overall intention in your journal. Next write your core intentions. Then write your immediate intentions. And finally, write your request/intent to receive help.

☐ Read your intentions upon awakening and before retiring. Allow yourself to feel the excitement...you have just committed to creating your dream life.

Note: Some of you will be able to write your intentions from the descriptions and samples in this chapter. Others might need a bit of extra help. For those who only know what they *don't* want, I have included a checklist and process to follow in Appendix A.

Desire

Energy

You create your own reality. You are a divine spark of consciousness - a part of God, a part of Goddess, a part of everything.

FIVE

BRINGING YOUR DREAM TO LIFE!

"The game of life is a game of boomerangs.
Our thoughts, deeds and words return to us
sooner or later with astounding accuracy."

—FLORENCE SCOVEL SHINN

Hopefully by now you are so excited you can hardly stand it! You have the beginning of a dream. And you have begun to let it sink in that you create every single bit of the world you call your own.

Wow, that is amazing isn't it?

But simply *knowing* you create your reality is not enough. And writing out your intentions is not enough...not if you want your dream in this lifetime. If you want to manifest something consciously, you must flow energy *towards* your desire and you must *stop* flowing energy away from that desire.

WHY FLOW ENERGY?

If you don't do anything suggested in this book you will *still* be creating your reality. Not by *making* things happen (consciously) but by *letting* things happen (unconsciously).

But if you *don't* consciously flow energy towards your intentions, nothing will change. You will get what you've always had—some good things and some bad things. This is what people call good and bad luck.

Imagine you are a car. And the fuel to get you to your destination (your desire) is energy (positive emotion).

The more fuel you put in and convert to movement, the faster you can go and the faster you get to your destination, right?

Except there is this opposing force in creation, let's call it anti-fuel or negativity.

Negativity neutralizes the fuel so that is it powerless. And if it is strong enough, it propels you backwards—further away from the thing you want.

To flow energy you need to *imagine* the thing you want and *feel* positive emotion about it at the same time. Things manifest when there is enough energy put towards that thing to make it "real." Flowing energy allows your dreams to come alive!

WHAT MAKES THE FLOW GROW?

Lots of things can make your flow grow (and your dreams manifest). I will teach you several techniques to increase the flow towards your dream in chapter seven.

But realize in every technique two critical components *must* exist:

1. You must think about having the thing you want (notice I did not say think about the thing...but think about *having* the thing—a subtle but important difference).

2. You must feel positive emotion (joy, excitement, peace, abundance, happiness, freedom, security, etc.) about having the thing you want.

Remember: both components must exist and emotion is the key!

But it isn't just what creates the flow that is important. Equally or even more important is...

WHAT STOPS THE FLOW?

Like gas in a car, the "flow" powers your dream to get you where you want to go. When the flow stops, you stop moving forward. And if anti-fuel or negativity enters the picture, you can even slide backwards, further away from your dream!

It is critical to become aware of what stops your flow. It often happens without your knowledge. But the more conscious you become, the easier it will be to avoid the flow-stoppers, get back on track, and flow energy towards your dreams again.

Remember, your emotions create your reality and negative emotions will create what you *don't* want. The flow-stopper emotions listed below don't always appear alone and sometimes they seem to be one emotion, like disappointment and doubt. I've listed them separately to make them easier to spot. So keep your eye out for:

SELF-PITY

It is impossible to be a powerful reality creator and a victim at the same time. If you find yourself feeling sorry for your-self—however minor or major the issue—stop. It is not serving you. Perhaps you like the attention in the form of pity from others, or it gives you a license to goof off and not get real, but be assured of this—it is screwing up your reality and you will only create more reasons to feel sorry for yourself.

ANTIDOTE FOR SELF-PITY:

Write a gratitude list. You can't feel sorry for yourself and feel grateful at the same time. Nothing to feel grateful for? Wow, you really are mired in self-pity! How about your hands—can you imagine yourself without those wonderful appendages? How about the beauty of the earth? How about the last person who smiled at you? How about this book? (I can hope, can't I?)

C'mon—force yourself to sit down and for three minutes, write down all the things you feel grateful for. See if you can come up with twenty-five things during those three minutes. And if it feels so good you want to keep going...spend twelve minutes and write one hundred reasons you have to feel grateful. And feel the gratitude, as fully as possible, while you are writing this list.

Then feel grateful for what you are *about* to receive from the universe. It will turn on the flow again like a faucet!

DOUBT

Doubt is the plague of dreams. It will take yours down and kill them before they even become baby realities. No matter what the doubt...that you have the ability to create what you want, that the universe can *deliver* what you want, that the details will fall into place despite the statistical odds...whatever it is, doubt is a dream-killer.

ANTIDOTE FOR DOUBT:

The antidote to doubt depends on how much of a problem your doubt becomes. Little doubts require little shifts. Constant and debilitating doubts require answers that delve deeper into the *why* of your doubt.

Fleeting doubt: The best way to handle fleeting doubt is to reinforce the dream or your ability to create the dream. You can keep track of your successes in conscious creation by noting each success in your journal. That way you can tap into the energy of your *past* successes and allow them to flow their energy into the *future*.

You could also read about others who have consciously created *their* realities or you might spend some time flowing energy to your dream (more about that in chapter seven).

Persistent doubt: Persistent doubt is doubt that happens so often or so intensely that it stops you from moving forward with your dream. When this happens, it is time to study your beliefs about your ability to consciously create. Do any of these beliefs sound or feel accurate to you?

- It is impossible to consciously create our own reality.
- It is impossible to consciously create *everything* in my reality.
- Conscious reality creation is impossible for *me*.
- It is hard work to consciously create my reality.
- It is impossible to create _____.
- I am not _____ enough to create what I desire.

If these or other beliefs are filling you with doubt about your ability to manifest a life you love, change them. It is easier than you think. I will teach you how to do this in the next chapter.

FEAR

Fear is one of the most debilitating flow-stoppers. Why? Most people cower in the face of fear. Or ignore it. Or pretend it doesn't exist. What happens then? Well, the fear just keeps flowing. And if it's flowing (e.g. you're feeling it even in the very back of your mind) you are creating more reasons to be fearful. Oh, it will not manifest quickly...negativity never does. But it *will* interfere with your dreams.

ANTIDOTE FOR FEAR:

The old adage "face your fears" is legit. Think about your fears and write them down. Play them out in your head. Decide what you will do if the worst fear does indeed happen and write that down.

Won't it make those things happen?

No. Ignoring your fears will give them energy to grow, but giving yourself (limited) time to face them and feel them will help you to release them. After you do this exercise, you'll find that the things you fear aren't so scary after all.

Also, some of our fears (many of our fears actually) are not really ours. They belong to our child, adolescent or younger adult selves. I will show you how to contact your younger selves and to give them what they need to feel safe later in this chapter.

You will be amazed at how many fears you *think* you have that really aren't *yours* and how easy it is to handle the fears of your younger selves. When you do, you will feel a huge shift in your confidence and excitement.

And finally, remember that fear comes up when you forget (or don't believe) the truth...that you are an eternal, divine being having a temporary "dream" experience. When you forget that you have created everything you fear, your fear can grow.

When you remember who you are, your fear dissipates.

Everyone experiences fear. It comes with the physical experience package. But it needn't interfere with your creations. Working with your fears will make a *huge* difference...handle them when they come up so you can truly let them go!

MARTYR

Do you ever feel overburdened? Do you ever feel that no one *gets* you? Do you ever feel that you've sacrificed something for someone who did not appreciate you? Hate to tell you this, since you kinda get off on feeling this way...but when you feel like that, you're being a martyr. And you're not just hurting the person you want to punish, but your own dreams, hopes and reality.

ANTIDOTE FOR MARTYR:

Just stop.

If you want to give, give. But don't give for any reason other than love and don't give with strings attached. The minute you expect someone to respond in any given way, you are no longer giving. You're hurting. If you don't want to give, don't. Don't sabotage your reality and hurt those you want to help by being a martyr. The key is to become *conscious* of your martyrdom. And stop.

CONTROL

We have been taught, from a very young age, to try to *control our world*. Our parents tried to control us. Our teachers did the same. We watched as our parents also tried to control each other, their jobs, their income and their families.

But control is a myth. Oh, we may *think* we have control over our lives. We may *think* that by taking precautions, we can control the outcome of any situation. But ultimately, control doesn't create realities. In fact, just the opposite is true.

We control when we fear that we won't get what we want, or that we will lose what we have. We control because we've been taught to believe that it's necessary to feel safe.

ANTIDOTE FOR CONTROL:

Notice when you try to control another person or situation. And stop. And remember your thoughts and feelings create your reality, not your control.

And if control continues to be a problem:

1. Change any constrictive beliefs you may hold, such as:

    "I must control others and my reality in order to be safe."

Or,

"I have to control to get what I want."

Change them to:

"I must create my own safety in order to be safe."

Or,

"I have to receive to get what I want."

2. Visit with your child or adolescent selves. Sometimes it isn't you, the adult who is afraid of what will happen if you lose control. Sometimes it's your younger selves. *They* may feel the need to control because they are afraid *they* won't be able to "do it right." Once you have worked with them to alleviate their fears (and given them the lives they want) they won't be dumping *their* fears into *your* life.

IMPATIENCE

We are impatient when we don't really believe we can create our own reality. If you *really* believed you could create every aspect of your life, you would be the most patient person in the world. Because you would realize that there is *nothing* to be impatient about. You would know that in time, every single wonderful thing you could ever imagine would manifest, *if you allow it*. And folks, allowing isn't passive. It's active. It's what this book is about.

ANTIDOTE FOR IMPATIENCE:

Remind yourself that things do not materialize instantly. Time lag causes a delay between the energy flow and the manifestation. Our dreams *do* take time to manifest fully. But they *will* manifest, *if* we allow them to.

Also, be alert for signs that your dreams are coming. Signs are proof that your energy is shifting. Signs will appear just hours or days after a powerful technique! You'll learn more about this in chapter nine.

It is also important to uncover any beliefs underlying your impatience, and to change them.

What might those beliefs look like? Something like this:
>*"I am not responsible for one hundred percent of my reality."*
>*"I am not powerful."*
>*"I cannot consciously create my entire world."*

Change them to:
>*"I am responsible for one hundred percent of my reality."*

"I am powerful."

"I can consciously create my entire world."

More on beliefs and how to change them in the next chapter.

JUDGMENT

Judging is different from having an opinion. An opinion says, *"This is what I like and this is what I don't like."* A judgment says, *"This is what I like and it is right and this is what I don't like and it is wrong."*

The minute you judge yourself or someone else, you are effectively telling your subconscious mind, *"I do not create everything in my world. Everything is not a reflection of my energy. Some of the things that others create are beyond my power and I am not safe."*

And the energy you are sending to others impacts them negatively. Judging hurts others and disempowers you.

ANTIDOTE FOR JUDGMENT:

Recognize what you are doing and the impact it has on yourself and others and consciously choose to stop judging.

Remember you are creating it all, consciously or unconsciously. There is no good or bad. There is only the illusion we call reality and we can experience either "good" or "bad" results from anything.

DISAPPOINTMENT

We feel disappointed when something doesn't work out the way we hoped. The check didn't come. The client didn't sign. The potential mate didn't call. The pounds weren't lost. The day didn't deliver what we thought it might.

When you feel disappointed, you are saying to your subconscious and the universe, *"I didn't get what I wanted."* What does that order for the future? Well, you may as well write the universe a note:

> *Please universe, no matter what I ask for, no matter what I say I want, don't deliver it to me. Because what I really want is to feel that "I never get what I want."*

And the universe, in its absolute, one hundred percent guaranteed compliance, says, *"No problem, babe. You want it, you got it!"* And it delivers *more* negative realities and again you feel that you don't get what you want. And on and on and on.

Underneath the disappointment is likely a fear and maybe, yes, a belief, that you will *never* get what you want. Obviously this is also *not* the energy you want to flow.

ANTIDOTE FOR DISAPPOINTMENT:

If you are disappointed don't, repeat don't, try to sweep it under the rug. If you *have* a disappointment, give yourself permission to *feel* it. Set a timer. Give yourself five minutes to feel deeply disappointed. Cry. Punch a pillow. Write about it. Do whatever it takes to release your feelings. But when the timer rings, stop.

It's important to remember that a disappointment does *not* mean you won't get your dream. A temporary setback is just that...temporary. Unless you *decide* it is permanent by accepting the disappointment as the end of the story.

Now it's time to forgive yourself and figure out *why* you created the disappointment:

1. Did you give yourself enough time? (Was the disappointment premature and is what you really need more patience?)

2. Do you have a belief that says you can't have it, can't create it or aren't worthy or deserving? Do you have a belief that says the responsibility of having the dream is too heavy? (Discover and change these.)

3. Did you let your child or adolescent self take over and are they the ones pushing it away? (You can work with them to make sure they're not flowing negative energy into your reality.)

There is *always* a reason for everything, folks. Always. And if there is a *reason* there is a *way* to *stop* putting forth that energy—and therefore change your world.

BLAME

Whenever you blame someone or something else for your reality, you are handing over your power to that person or thing on a silver platter. Is the economy responsible for you losing your job? You have given the economy your power. Is your spouse responsible for your bankruptcy? You have given your spouse power over your finances.

ANTIDOTE FOR BLAME:

Stop blaming. It's a habit. Break the habit.

Every time you find yourself starting to blame, repeat, *"I hereby absolve everyone and everything from blame. I take my power back from all those I have given it to and I intend to create a life I love in every regard. I now ask that my unseen friends help me to take responsibility for my life and to guide and assist me in creating a life I love."*

ENTITLEMENT

Have you ever felt that you *should* have received more for your hard work? Have you ever felt that someone "owed" you? This is entitlement and it will stop your flow every time. Why?

Entitlement tells the universe, *"I have earned this."* And guess what?

The universe doesn't care. The universe responds to flow—thoughts, feelings and beliefs. The feeling you are emitting with entitlement is, *"I don't have what I want and I should."* It's a little bit different from, *"I have what I want and I'm grateful,"* isn't it?

The only thing entitlement creates is more reasons to feel entitled.

ANTIDOTE FOR ENTITLEMENT:

Become good at recognizing entitlement. And cut it out. No one owes you anything, unless you are five years old. Take responsibly for your life and stop looking to others to provide what you want.

GUILT

Guilt is a bit more complex, and it may come up for you more now than before you knew how to consciously create. You may think, *"I shouldn't have a beautiful life because (my sister, my husband, my father, my best friend, the people in*

Africa…) don't have a beautiful life."

Guilt will *stop* your positive flow of energy if you let it.

ANTIDOTE FOR GUILT:

Realize that the best thing you could *ever* do for those you love and care about is to create a life of your dreams. Why?

1. Staying at a lesser vibration for those you love doesn't really help them and it hurts you too.
2. If you shift to a higher resonance they can follow you there with a map you created.
3. They may be staying at a lower vibration as a gift to you—and once you choose to move higher and create a more self-loving reality, they may be freed to go ahead and create it too.

JEALOUSY

Before we realize that we create our own reality, it's easy to feel jealous of other people. Jealously says, *"You have what I want and I don't."* Jealousy denies that we have a choice. Jealousy forgets the fact that we create it all.

ANTIDOTE FOR JEALOUSY:

Remind yourself that not only do you create it all, you have created the *person you are jealous of.* And the fact that you have created someone having what you want is a "sign" that you can have it too! *Celebrate* others having what you want! It is an indication that the same realities are closer than ever to you (if you don't let jealousy get the better of you, that is)!

SHAME

Shame says, "*I am flawed. I am inherently defective. And because something is wrong with me, I do not deserve to live a life I love.*" Everyone who has been physically, mentally or emotionally abused carries shame. If you carry shame, you will allow yourself to create some, but not all of your dreams until you heal it.

ANTIDOTE FOR SHAME:

Shame is not just about choice. The spiritual teacher Lazaris,[1] advises that shame must be given back to the person(s) who dumped it on you. To accomplish this, simply go into a meditation or visualization and hand those who have shamed you a big bag of "shame." Tell them it is not yours, and you will no longer carry it.

In addition, I would suggest that you enlist the assistance of

---

1   Lazaris has compiled a brilliant series of audio cds on ending shame and I recommend them for those who feel drawn to do this work. www.lazaris.com

your unseen friends to help you in this work. If the feeling of being "flawed" does not seem to lift, there are books on this subject and therapists who specialize in the healing of shame. As someone who has dealt with this issue in depth, I can tell you, it *is* healable.

If you keep an eye out for these flow-stoppers you will be well on your way to becoming a stellar creator.

WHO IS FLOWING WHAT?

Guess what? The adult, present-time you is not the only one flowing energy!

WORKING WITH YOUR CHILD, ADOLESCENT AND YOUNG ADULT SELVES

You understand that flowing energy in the form of thoughts, feelings and beliefs will create the world around you. But you've probably not given much thought as to what *part* of you is doing the flowing.

We are complex beings. Even though our bodies have grown older, we haven't lost the child "us," the adolescent "us" or even the young adult "us." Because we know that time and space are an illusion, our child, adolescent and young adult selves *still* exist. We grow older, but that wounded child and scared adolescent are still within us.

And these other parts of "us" can put out energy *towards*, or in *opposition to* our dreams. This is why it is critical to spend time with our younger selves to be certain that *their* energy is in alignment with where we, the conscious adult, wants to go.

I began to work with my child and adolescent selves over two decades ago. I was introduced to this work by Lazaris[2], and it *literally* changed my life. I finally understood why I sometimes sabotaged my creations. I learned how to contact my younger selves and ferret out *their* limiting beliefs, which were also *my* limiting beliefs.

The more I worked with my younger selves, the easier it was to manifest what I wanted. My younger selves were no longer flowing their own thoughts, emotions and beliefs into my reality. For example, when I started my own business at age forty, the-five-year old "me" was petrified.

Why?

Because she was *incapable* of running a company. No wonder she was petrified—what five-year-old can run a company?

But I was able to go to her, and assure her that *I* could run a

---

2   Lazaris details working with the child and adolescent in much deeper ways than I do in this book. I highly recommend their CDs and seminars on these as well as other subjects. For more information visit www.lazaris.com

company just fine. I gave her what she wanted: safety, security, parents who loved and took care of her, and a merry-go-round in her backyard (I never judge what she wants!). And although she was the one whose fear was eliminated, "I" felt the relief.

I also listened carefully to the "fears" of my five-year-old self. What did she tell me?

> *"It's hard to run a business."*
> *"You have to work and work and work to make a business grow."*
> *"You probably won't make much money at your business."*
> *"You can't make money doing what you love."*

Why did I listen so carefully? Because *she believed* these things. And if my five-year-old believed them, *I also* believed them. Even though I simultaneously held beliefs that were quite the opposite at the very same time.

I wrote down what she said, and I changed these beliefs:

> *"It's hard to run a business."*
> *"You have to sacrifice yourself to make a business grow."*
> *"Small businesses can't make you rich."*
> *"You can't make money doing what you love."*

to:

> *"It's easy to run a business."*
> *"You have to be passionate to make a business grow."*
> *"Small businesses can make you rich."*
> *"You can make money doing what you love."*

And I was *then* able to create the business success I dreamed of.

WORKING WITH YOUR CHILD SELF

Let's assume your dream is to have a beautiful home, a job you love and plenty of money. And let's assume that when you were a child, you were playing at your grandmother's home one day, and you asked for seconds on ice cream. And your grandmother scolded you for being greedy, and "never being satisfied with what you have."

That simple little statement may have entrenched a belief that says:

> *"It is selfish to want more than I have,"* or

> *"Wanting more means I am greedy,"* or

> *"I can have a little bit but never everything I want,"* or even,

> *"I'm not worthy of having what I want."*

Sometimes the littlest comments can cause a child to make blanket assumptions about the entire nature of their reality. And if your child self is flowing energy *away* from your dream rather than *towards* it, you have a problem.

A TECHNIQUE TO CONNECT WITH YOUR CHILD SELF

Find a quiet spot. Play soft music and sit with your eyes closed. Relax your body and quiet your mind. Then imagine the house you lived in when you were five years old.

See the sky, the earth, the clouds, the colors, the textures. Hear the birds singing, the breeze blowing. Feel the warmth of the sun on your skin. Smell the day—the earth, the flowers, the subtle scents of long ago. Even taste the place that so many years ago, you called home.

And go to that small person who is you at four, five or six years old. Find that child. They will be alone, in solitude. For some part of that child knows you will be coming.

And just sit with that child. Explain who you are, *"I am a future you. I am here to visit with you. I love you."*

And listen to them. Hear what they have to say. Ask them about their life.

And when it feels right, tell them about your dream. Tell them about the thing that is most important to you right now, your number-one intention.

And listen to what they have to say.

It may be something like, *"You can't trust a (wo)man...don't you remember what mom/dad said about that?"* or *"You are crazy, you can't make things happen like magic!"* or they may warn you about the downside of having this dream. *"Once you get the money everyone is going to try and take it away from you...that's what people do."*

And when they have finished, tell them the best news ever!

"I am not only from your future," you say, *"but I have magical abilities not only in my own life but in yours too! I can instantly change your world, in the blink of an eye!"*

It's not likely that your child self will believe you. So show them. Give them whatever they want. Don't assume you know. Ask them.

And if they want a money machine so money is never a problem again, give it to them.

If they want a different mommy and daddy...parents that make them feel loved, and who don't work, and who will spend all day with them...give it to them.

If they want a Ferris wheel in the back yard, give it to them!

"What? Won't I spoil them?"

No. You will make them extremely happy. And they will stay in *their* world, happily ever after, while you are free to go back to *yours* and manifest the life you want, without their interference.

And once you've created this magical life for your child self, tell them, *"Now you stay here in your world, and have a blast, while I go back to mine. I will be back to see you. But I need you to stay here."* They won't have a problem with this, since you've filled them with a sense of safety and made their world so much fun.

This work will also be fun for *you*. You will *feel* the shift in your own energy and *see* changes in your life after you've done this work. Suddenly your dream will feel more believable and more exciting than ever!

WORKING WITH YOUR ADOLESCENT SELF

Your adolescent self is also a real part of you, even now. It has a different take on life and different beliefs than your child self. And your adolescent self is also flowing energy away from your dreams. Until you do something about it.

And what can you do? A lot.

You can take your power back from your adolescent self, you can give her/him the reality she/he desires, and you can hugely strengthen the flow you are sending out towards your dream. You will see the difference in your reality.

Follow the same technique as with your child self. Remember adolescence is a very dramatic period of time. Everything is life or death and black and white to an adolescent. We strive to discover who we are in these years and be accepted by those we value. A perceived hurt during this time can vastly color our outlook on life and its possibilities.

With one look from another across a crowded room your adolescent may have decided life was too painful! You were unlovable! Love hurts! Or any of a million beliefs. Take some time. Hang out with your adolescent. He or she may be flowing a lot more energy into your reality than you *ever* imagined.

Case in point: I had a rather easy adolescence, as I look back on it. I was fairly popular, pretty, smart and talented. But that wasn't my adolescent's viewpoint. She was inse-cure, scared and felt like she was never enough—not smart enough, rich enough, popular enough, clever enough or cute enough.

And I didn't realize until I started working with her that she was keeping me from a lot of the things I wanted as an adult. So what did I do? I talked with her to understand her beliefs, so I could change them, and then I gave her everything she wanted in her reality.

I gave her:

A money machine. She only had to push a button and twenty-dollar bills came out. She could do that over and over again, as many times as she wanted, whenever she wanted.

A beautiful house to live in circa 1970 "Brady Bunch" style. Replete with an Olympic-sized swimming pool and a maid named Alice.

Smokin' hot boyfriends who changed according to her mood. (But she was always pursued by the heartthrob of her time...Davy Jones! Yes, I'm *that* old.)

A job as the world's most popular supermodel (despite the fact that she stands only 5'4" tall), complete with private jets and incredibly hip stylists.

Patient and loving parents who wanted nothing more than her complete and total happiness.

A bevy of BFFs to swoon over her mega-success and giggle with at sleepovers and red carpet events.

What adolescent girl of the 70s era *wouldn't* be at peace and in joy with a life like that?

Exactly.

If your adolescent self is at peace and in joy, then he or she isn't messing with *your* reality.

And remember, the objections of both your child and adolescent selves have likely become beliefs, so don't let this work end here. Jot down what they say, and if they reveal constrictive beliefs, change them with the techniques I'll give you in the next chapter. When you do, your reality *will* shift.

WORKING WITH YOUR YOUNG (AND OLDER) ADULT SELVES

Your younger adult selves also had some dreams die. Failures have accumulated. They may have a dire outlook on life and be less than enchanted with what life has to offer. *Their* outlooks, experiences and beliefs are flowing energy into *your* world.

What can you do about that? Plenty. Spend some time with the "you" who experienced major disappointments in life. These disappointments may have been decades ago, or as recently as last month. It doesn't matter.

What *does* matter is that job you didn't get, the love affair that went sour, the investment that never paid off or the friend who betrayed you. These disappointments are affecting *your* ability to manifest your dreams *today*.

Go back and talk with that younger "you." Encourage your younger self to *feel* the disappointment. Let him or her cry, rant, rave, shout and blow up the world if they want to. Encourage your younger self to *release* the emotions.

Then...give that younger self what it wanted. Let him or her marry their lover *before* it went sour. Let that self *get* the job. Let the investment pay more than expected. Let your younger self have the most *loyal* friend in the world.

The scars from that younger self are stopping *your* dreams. And you can heal that. Very, very simply. Just give that self what it wanted.

Are you kidding? When I was that age I wanted to be a multi-billionaire. I wanted my coffee shop idea to be a worldwide franchise! It was ridiculous!

It doesn't matter how wild your dreams were at that age. Give it to that self. Allow that self to feel how she or he would feel if *all their* dreams had come true!

A marriage failed? Go back to that adult self and dream it succeeding.

But I don't want it to succeed!

Of course not. You are past it. But the person you were when you married *did* want it to succeed. *That self* had a dream. *That self* thinks it failed. That failure energy is being "flowed" through you—24/7.

You can hugely empower yourself by going back to your younger selves and revising *their* lives. Imagine all of the dreams, through all of your life, coming true! You will be absolutely amazed at the impact this has on *your* world.

And there is one more "you" who flows energy, like it or not...

YOUR DARK SIDE: YOUR NEGATIVE SELF

There is a darker side of you, whom I call the negative self, who, plain and simple, wants to see you fail and says whatever it can to see that you do. The negative self is the part of you that represents your inner saboteur, your inner critic and your ego's negative aspect. This is the least evolved part of your being. This self speaks to you through your thoughts and feelings and it can have a huge negative impact on your dreams.

The negative self speaks lies of less-than. This is the part of you that haunts you in the middle of the night. This is the part of you that tells you you'll fail, that you aren't talented, you aren't attractive or good enough.

It also speaks lies of better-than. It tells you that you are the "exception." You are "special." You are God's "gift" to humankind.

It will fill your head with so much garbage, so many lies, so much self doubt and debilitating nonsense day in and day out that if you aren't careful, you will begin to believe it. And if you don't start to differentiate your "true self" from your "negative self," you will have a very hard time manifesting a life you love, or even a life you kinda like.

When I first began to give voice to this negative aspect of myself, I was shocked at how brutal and incapacitating it was. I began to see how critical it was to give my negative self a voice, ironically because that was the only way to silence its impact.

Here is what my negative self had to say years ago at a time when I was trying to manifest both monetary abundance and a loving relationship:

> Me: *"I am planning to create financial independence and also a relationship with someone who supports, honors and nurtures me."*

> NS: *"You don't deserve money and you'll never have money. You think you can do some stupid technique and money will fall in your lap? What kind of turnip truck did you fall from? You are stupid to believe that. Idiotic. The best you will be able to do is to work for*

*someone else and what can you make doing what
you know how to do? Not much. Give it up."*

NS: *"And as far as a man...you can't be serious...what
kind of man would want you? Blind? Stupid? An imbe-
cile? Forget it, baby. This is your lifetime to be alone."*

Me: *"Is that all?"*

NS: *"No. I can't believe you are trying this "you create your own reality" crap again. It if really worked,
wouldn't it have worked by now?"*

Me: *"Are you finished?"*

NS: *"Actually no. You won't have men or money this
time around, sweet cakes. So just stop trying. You are
ugly and stupid and no man will want you. And as
far as being rich, it just ain't in the cards."*

Me: *"Anything else?"*

NS: *"Yeah, that dress you bought makes you look fat."*

Me: *"Now are you done?"*

Nothing from my negative self, so I assumed it was
finished. I imagined surrounding it in a bubble of
white light, and called in my higher self to take her to

be healed.

And then, I was free. Until next time.

WORKING WITH YOUR NEGATIVE SELF

In order to stop your negative self from flowing *its* night-mares into *your* dreams, you have to become aware of it. The best way to do that is to dialogue, just like I did (this is based on a similar technique that Lazaris[3] teaches about working with the negative ego). To do this, get into a comfortable position in a quiet place where you will not be interrupted. Put on some soft music. Light a candle if you like. You are creating a resonance for inner work.

Then imagine your negative self coming up to you and sit-ting beside you. I imagine my negative self as me on a very bad day. She's wearing a dirty and ripped sweat suit, with hair that hasn't been washed in days. She's always slouching, snarly and smelly. You can imagine yours looking like you, or completely different. Do whatever works for you.

And then simply tell it what you are trying to heal, manifest or change in your life. And let it talk. That's it. Just let it talk. When it is finished, call in the unseen friend of your choice, to take it away for love and healing. And then just open your eyes.

Once you are aware of it you can diffuse its power. Sometimes,

3   www.lazaris.com

what the negative self says can make you aware of a belief you hold. Sometimes, it's all just words. But after you've let it have its say, and have sent it off with an unseen friend for healing, you will feel awesome—light, clear and free.

Whenever I have a big or new project or dream, I work with my negative self daily. It doesn't have to be meditative; you can talk to it in your head (after a bit of practice) in the car or the shower or anyplace that works for you.

Even now, after years of working with my negative self, it can *still* throw me for a loop *if* I ignore it. Working with it has had a profound impact on my life and I will likely never stop. I suggest you don't either.

WHEN SHOULD YOU WORK WITH YOUR "SELVES"?

In the beginning work with them all, one by one, and get acquainted. They will be extremely helpful in discovering the beliefs you didn't know you held.

After that, I suggest that you work with your younger selves every time you dream a new dream. With practice you will begin to know when they need help and attention. One clue is that you begin to act like them—a scared child, an egotistical adolescent, or a know-it-all young adult.

I suggest that you work with your negative self daily for at least three months. It is critical that you begin to know when your negative self is speaking, and by working with it daily you will learn to recognize its voice in your head. Again, it doesn't have to take more than a few minutes in the shower. After that, work with your negative self when you dream a new dream, or make a big change in your life. It may seem like a lot of work at first, but the results will amaze you.

THE BIGGER PICTURE: ALIGNING ALL YOUR ENERGY

Why do we work with these selves? We work with them to make certain that *all* of our energy is in alignment with our dreams.

When this happens, you'll be able to consciously flow energy towards your desires without interference. This will allow you to manifest your dreams more quickly.

However, becoming conscious of every single aspect of who you are is daunting, if not impossible. How do we align the "flow" of all of our selves in an easy, straightforward way? We work with our beliefs.

In the next chapter you'll discover how to work *real* magic with your reality! You will learn to access your subconscious mind and *permanently* change your beliefs, and thus, your world.

LIFE-ALTERING TAKE AWAYS

Read these slowly. Meditate on them or sit and contemplate them. Let them in. Let them change you.

* *Knowing* you create your reality is not enough. If you want to manifest something consciously, you must flow energy *towards* your desire and you must *stop* flowing energy *away* from that desire.

* Realize in *every* technique two critical components *must* exist:

  1. You must think about *having* the thing you want (notice I did not say think about the thing...but think about *having* the thing—a subtle but important difference).

  2. You must feel positive emotion (joy, excitement, peace, abundance, happiness, freedom, security, etc.) about having the thing you want.

* Even though our bodies have grown older, we haven't lost the child "us," the adolescent "us" or even the young adult "us." These other parts of "us" can flow energy towards, or in opposition to our dreams. This is why it is critical to spend time with these aspects of ourselves to be certain their energy is in alignment with where we, the conscious adult wants to go.

✦ You also have a less evolved, scared and self-sabotaging part of you who wants to take you down. I call this the "negative self." But don't worry...once you are aware of its existence you can eliminate its influence over you and your dreams.

✦ When *all* of your energy is in alignment with your dreams, it will become easier to consciously flow energy towards your desires. This will allow you to manifest your dreams more quickly.

YOUR NEXT STEPS

☐ What flow-stoppers can you identify? What triggers them? Become comfortable with the antidote and intend to use it the next time one of these emotions comes up for you.

☐ Work with your child, adolescent and young adult. Ask them how they feel about your becoming proficient at creating your reality. Do they have any objections? Fears? Questions? Write them down in your journal. We will come back to these fears in the next chapter.

☐ Work with your negative self. Let it know you are becoming a masterful magician in your world. Let it rant and rave and tell you how you will fail. Leave it with your higher self for healing.

SIX

THE 24/7 FLOW: BELIEFS

*"My life is mine and I form it. Tell yourself this often.
Create your own life now, using your beliefs as an artist uses color."*

—SETH

Beliefs, beliefs, beliefs...you'd have to be a hermit to have not heard an earful about beliefs during your lifetime. But people, there is a *reason* you've heard a lot about beliefs.

Beliefs control your world.

I am not being dramatic here. They do. And do you know the worst part?

Given the nature of beliefs, it is difficult to see the impact they have. You don't see them as *mutable*. You see them as "life," as the "way it is." As unchangeable as the earth and the sky.

You are skeptical about changing them. And you are reluctant to change them. You are stuck.

How do you get beyond the stuck? Faith. Faith in that "something" deep within you that knows there is more. Faith in something says, *"It will be worth it."*

I don't think anyone has ever changed their first belief really expecting it to change. But that's OK. You don't need to expect it. You just have to be willing to try the exercise.

How do beliefs work? When I talk about the flow of thoughts and feelings creating your reality, you can imagine how powerful those thoughts and feelings must be, right? Well, imagine a thought and feeling that you thought and felt 24/7. *That* is a belief.

These are thoughts and feelings that are wired into your system. These are thoughts and feelings that are so solid you take them as absolute truth. And you emit that energy, which in turn creates your reality, one hundred percent of the time.

Yes, beliefs are that solid. That impactful. That important.

When you change your beliefs you literally change your world. Your success. Your finances. Your health. Your relationships. *Everything* changes.

CLEARING THE WAY FOR BELIEF WORK

To discover the beliefs that are playing a part in creating your reality, you must be calm, centered and as detached as possible. Why?

Because belief work is subtle, delicate work. You will be relying on your gut, ultimately, to tell you whether you have hit upon a belief or not. And if you are angry or upset, you won't be able to tell what your beliefs really are.

What type of emotions might need to be released? Whatever keeps you from being in a calm and centered state, especially around the area of life you are working on. For instance:

> *Maybe you desire to create a job but you were just laid off from your last job yesterday. You might need to express and release feelings of anger, hurt and sadness.*

Maybe you desire to create a relationship but your partner cheated on you in the last one. You might need to express and let go of the feelings of rage, betrayal and hurt.

Maybe you desire to create more money but you once tried to start your own multi-level marketing business and lost more money than you made. You might need to express and let go of your feelings of failure, disappointment and fear.

Maybe you desire to create a promotion at work but your boss passed you over for the last one. You might need to express and let go of your anger or self-pity, or feelings of betrayal, entitlement or disappointment.

Even if your upset is not connected to what you desire to create, you still need to come to your belief work with a calm, centered spirit. So take a moment and ask yourself if you have something you need to let go of. If you do, take a few minutes to express it.

How?

There are a myriad of ways to release emotions. But one of my favorites is to write a *hate letter*.

Now, please understand...you don't write a hate letter because you wish anyone harm. You write it in order to *release the constrictive emotions of anger, rage, betrayal, etc.*

Now THIS is important—*you do not need to give anyone the letter!* This exercise is for the purpose of clearing emotions only. If it's appropriate to share your feelings with someone, write *another* letter after you've released the intensity of your emotions.

Write this hate letter to someone who you feel has done you wrong, or to yourself, your higher self, or even to God.

Write a hate letter to God?

Yes. To God. Our emotions are not always rational. Even though we may know God didn't want something bad to happen in our lives, part of us may still blame Him. And in order to get to the belief that would create that reality, those emotions need to be expressed.

And folks, God doesn't take it personally. Unconditional love is unconditional. And He's all for you getting to the bottom of whatever it is that stops you from living the life you were born to live.

So pour out your feelings. Swear. Call them names. Make it strong. *Feel* your feelings fully as you write. If you finish the letter and your negative emotions are not fully spent, put it away until the next day you do this work and then make it stronger.

When your emotions have been released (for now—this does not mean you will never feel them again but it's a good start), burn the letter (safely, in the kitchen sink, a metal bowl or the fireplace).

Then forgive yourself. Forgive yourself for creating this reality and for anything else you feel you did wrong. Holding onto self-blame will keep you stuck in old and punishing realities forever, if you let it.

From there, you're free to move on to...

DISCOVERING YOUR BELIEFS

It's likely you have thousands of beliefs. And you're unaware of the vast majority of them. And that's fine. There's no reason you need to become aware of most of your beliefs, because they support realities you want to keep.

But in the areas of life you want to change, it's important to *uncover* the beliefs that hold those realities in place. It will take some detective work to uncover the beliefs that create what you don't want, so where do you begin? You begin by *paying attention*.

You pay attention to:

What you think.
What you feel.

What you say.
What you do.
What you create.

WHAT YOU *THINK* IS A CLUE
ABOUT YOUR BELIEFS

When I say pay attention to what you think, I am not suggesting you monitor every thought. That would be incredibly difficult, if not impossible. I am suggesting that you pay attention to your thoughts about a particular issue.

For example:

Let's say you want to create a beautiful and healthy body, with ease and elegance. And you notice that some of your thoughts around food and your body are:

> *I'd better not eat that cookie. I'll get fatter than I already am.*
> *The bathing suit I tried on makes me look like a house.*
> *God, I'm looking haggard and old.*
> *I wonder if I could fast tomorrow...that would give me a kick start on losing ten pounds.*

And those thoughts could indicate the beliefs you want to change. What beliefs might you hold in this example? They might be:

I am fat.
I look old and haggard.
I have no control over whether I age.
I must deprive myself in order to lose weight.
I must lose weight in order to be beautiful.
I should look great in any clothing I put on.
I am not beautiful.
I can't eat what I want and look the way I want.
Extra calories make me gain weight.

Wait a minute...but extra calories do make me gain weight! I hear you say.

Of course they do. If that is what you believe. Yet look around. Not everyone holds that belief. And their bodies are proof.

WHAT YOU *FEEL* IS A CLUE ABOUT YOUR BELIEFS

Again, you don't have to monitor every single feeling. What you do need to pay attention to, however, are the bad feelings that relate to the thing you *want* to create.

For example:

Let's say you have an illness or disease and you want to create vibrant health in every part of your body. Yet every time you think of your malady, or when it's time to take your medicine (be it traditional or alternative), you feel fear *and dread* in the pit of your stomach.

The first step, of course, is noticing that fear. The next step is asking yourself why you are afraid. These might be the answers in this example:

> *What if I've put my faith in the wrong system?*
> *What if I've chosen the wrong doctor?*
> *What if this "medicine" makes me sick?*
> *What if this "medicine" creates more problems than it cures?*
> *What if this doesn't work?*
> *What if I die?*

And what beliefs might these fears point to?

> *I cannot trust myself.*
> *Medical doctors cannot heal me.*
> *Alternative doctors cannot heal me.*
> *I make poor choices.*
> *Medicine is poison.*
> *I am powerless around the issue of my health.*

Your emotions are a tremendous resource in this work. Trust them. They exist for a reason and have great gifts for you.

WHAT YOU *SAY* IS A CLUE
ABOUT YOUR BELIEFS

Your words create. And they are tattletales. They reveal your beliefs to others before you're even aware of what you said. How many times have you heard people utter words such as these:

> *I can't afford it.*
> *There are no jobs in this economy.*
> *When you get to be my age there are no single men/ women to be found.*
> *Your body falls apart after thirty (or forty, or fifty, or whatever).*
> *Just when you get ahead something happens to put you back behind.*
> *Life's a bitch, and then you die.*

These aren't just common clichés. They are indicative of deeply held beliefs. What beliefs might they be showing you? Consider these:

> *There is limited abundance available.*
> *The world I live in is real and beyond my control.*
> *The economy is responsible for the state of my finances.*
> *I cannot create my love life.*
> *My body must age and deteriorate as I get older.*
> *Life is difficult and meaningless.*

Also be aware of what the people around you say. Time

after time you will see that what people say is indicative of what they believe. And what they believe is what they create. Those who complain create more to complain about. Those who are abundant in money or love create more of the same. Of course you won't see all of everyone's beliefs by listening closely. But you will see some and it will strengthen your knowing of how this universe works.

It's also fun to look at what famous people throughout history have said about the nature of reality. It's not surprising that many successful people spoke of and believed in a responsive universe. Here are just a few:

> **Albert Einstein:** *"Reality is merely an illusion, albeit a very persistent one."*

> **Buddha:** *"We are what we think. All that we are arises with our thoughts. With our thoughts we make the world."*

> **Carl Jung:** *"What you resist persists."*

> **Charles Fillmore:** *"The spiritual substance from which comes all visible wealth is never depleted. It is right with you all the time and responds to your faith in it and your demands on it."*

> **Charles Haanel:** *"The predominant thought or the mental attitude is the magnet, and the law is that like*

attracts like, consequently, the mental attitude will invariably attract such conditions as correspond to its nature."

Edgar Allen Poe: "*All that we see or seem is but a dream within a dream.*"

James Allen: "*You are today where your thoughts have brought you; you will be tomorrow where your thoughts take you.*"

Jim Carrey: "*I made myself [out a] check which was just basically...ten million dollars to Jim Carrey for acting services rendered, dated Thanksgiving 1995, and that was...1990. I gave myself five years to be one of the most successful working actors, to be given the best material, and the best scripts— things that people would never expect in a million years that I could do.*"

Ralph Waldo Emerson: "*Great men are they who see that spiritual is stronger than any material force, that thoughts rule the world.*"

Kahlil Gibran: "*Poverty hides itself in thought before it surrenders to purses.*"

Madonna: "*A lot of people are afraid to say what they want. That's why they don't get what they want.*"

Mohandas K. Gandhi: *"A man is but a product of his thoughts; what he thinks, that he becomes."*

Oprah, on her show about the *The Secret,* the DVD and book about the law of attraction and conscious reality creation: *"I didn't know it was a secret!"*

Ralph Waldo Emerson: *"The good news is that the moment you decide that what you know is more important than what you have been taught to believe, you will have shifted gears in your quest for abundance. Success comes from within, not from without."*

Robert Collier: *"See the things that you want as already yours. Know that they will come to you as need. Then let them come. Don't fret and worry about them. Don't think about your lack of them. Think of them as yours, as belonging to you, as already in your possession."*

Shirley MacLaine: *"I have learned, profoundly, in my life that I create my own reality every minute of the day and night."*

W. Clement Stone: *"Whatever the mind can conceive it can achieve."*

William James: *"The greatest discovery of my generation is that a human being can alter his life by* *altering his attitudes of mind."*

Winston Churchill: *"You create your own universe as you go along."*

I have been fascinated with biographies of rich, famous and even downtrodden people since I discovered that we create our own reality. From these books—and especially the auto-biographies—you can see clearly in words and actions, what people believed. And without fail, they created what they thought, felt and believed. Real life stories show it so clearly!

So listen to what you say! Not only because words have power, but they may also be a signpost to your beliefs.

And if someone in your life can help you to become conscious of your words, all the better. Ask someone you trust and who understands this work to listen to what you say and (gently) point out when you say something that is not in alignment with what you want. Others can often catch what we cannot.

WHAT YOU *DO* IS A CLUE ABOUT YOUR BELIEFS

How does this show up? It shows up something like this:

You say you want to learn to create your own reality but you don't do the exercises (or even finish the book!).

Your beliefs might be:
> *It is impossible to create my own reality.*
> *These techniques won't work.*
> *I am not powerful.*
> *This may work for others, but not for me.*

You *say* you want to improve your marriage but you keep picking at it and your partner.

Your beliefs might be:
> *I cannot change my marriage without changing my partner.*
> *I cannot create a loving and respectful partnership.*
> *I am not worthy of a wonderful, loving relationship.*

You *say* you want to learn to be a successful writer but instead of writing you watch another movie.

Your beliefs might be:
> *I am not good enough to make my living by writing.*
> *It is impossible to create success with my writing.*
> *It is not possible to make a lot of money doing what you love.*
> *It will take years if not decades to become well known enough to make money at writing.*

You *say* you want to go back to school but you keep putting it off for one more semester.

Your beliefs might be:

> *I am not smart enough to succeed at college.*
> *I am not disciplined enough to succeed at college.*
> *I am not motivated or organized enough to succeed at college.*
> *A college degree won't be worth what it takes to achieve it.*

You *say* you want to learn to create a loving partnership but you never leave your house.

Your beliefs might be:

> *I will never find a loving partner.*
> *There aren't any good men/women out there.*
> *I am not good enough to be loved by someone I love.*
> *I am not pretty/handsome enough to be loved by someone I love.*
> *I am not young enough to be loved by someone I love.*

You say you want to increase your financial abundance, but you play video games instead of looking for those limiting beliefs.

Your beliefs might be:

> *There is only so much money.*
> *Abundance is limited.*
> *Maybe others can create money but not me.*
> *I only have so much control over my reality.*
> *Changing beliefs won't change my reality.*

Please recognize that beliefs may not be the only thing going on here. There are a lot of reasons that people say one thing and do another.

The would-be college student may not be clear about what he/she wants to do or study. The disgruntled spouse may not want to improve his/her marriage because they don't even *like* their spouse. The single guy/gal may not want a mate, but because they think they should, they keep *saying* they do.

What you *say, think, feel and do* are all rather small clues as to what your beliefs might be. However...

WHAT YOU *CREATE* IS THE BIGGEST CLUE OF ALL ABOUT YOUR BELIEFS

You can tell me all day long how much you *believe* that you create your reality. But what does your *reality* say? The absolute best way of discovering your beliefs is to look at what you have already created. You may deceive yourself—or be unconscious of the truth—but your reality never lies. *It* reflects as clear as day what you really, deep down, truly *believe*.

Let's look at a few examples of realities showing what someone probably believes:

Mary's reality:

"I never have a problem attracting men who want to date

me. They come into my life, but when we get close and I commit to them in my heart, they disappoint me in some way and I realize that they aren't who I thought they were. I really want a committed, loving partnership."

Mary's reality is showing her these possible beliefs:

> *Men are untrustworthy.*
> *Men always disappoint me.*
> *I can't trust my heart when it comes to men.*
> *I can't have a truly loving and committed relationship.*
> *It is a struggle to create a loving relationship.*
> *There are no good men out there.*
> *A good man wouldn't love me.*
> *Love hurts.*

In addition, this reality may point to core beliefs such as:

> *I don't deserve.*
> *I am not good enough.*
> *I am unworthy.*

George's reality:

"Although I'm doing well financially I'm not where I want to be! I'm currently (barely) making all my bills, but I want to make more money! I don't feel that money comes easily to me like it does for other people. But then some weeks I feel

like it does and everything is good again. I need to figure out how to keep it that way.

My brain doesn't seem to ever stop thinking and I'm constantly coming up with new ideas! But I think I'm doing too much thinking and not enough doing (even though I still work sixty hours a week). I know I have good things coming in the future but it's hard to be patient."

George's reality is showing him these possible beliefs:

> *Money is difficult to create.*
> *Life and/or money is a struggle.*
> *You have to earn money.*
> *You must be ever vigilant in creating money.*
> *No matter how much I make, there is never enough.*

In addition, this reality may point to core beliefs such as:

> *I don't deserve.*
> *I am not enough.*
> *I am flawed.*

The beliefs above may seem obvious. Yet when it comes to our own beliefs, we are often blinded by our emotions and too close to the situation. When you look at your own reality, try to be as detached as possible. And asking yourself three very precise questions will help immensely.

BELIEF DISCOVERY: THREE CRITICAL QUESTIONS

Ask yourself these questions when you are looking for your beliefs:

1. What do I *want*?
2. What do I *have*?
3. What would someone *have* to believe to have created what I did?

Here is an example of how this might look for an issue with children:

What do I want?

> *I want peace and total freedom around my children. I want to stop enabling them. I want to add positive energy to their creations of success by seeing them as powerful, strong, wise, happy and successful.*

What do I have?

> *A son who expects me to take responsibility for everything in his life. A son who will punish me for the parts of his life that are not working—and it is all not working. And I have a daughter who will use illness/ accidents as a way to make me pay.*

I am preoccupied and sad about their choices. I'm sad about not being with them. Yet when I'm with them, it's often hell. They keep me from moving forward in my own life and enjoying fully the beautiful life I have created.

What would one have to believe to have created such a reality?

I am responsible for my children in every way.
If something does not work in my children's lives it is ultimately my fault.
I must suffer if my children suffer.
I must be punished because I am a bad mother.
My children cannot survive unless I take responsibility for them.
My adult children are young, innocent and vulnerable.
My children are unable to be successful in the world.
I can't love my children without feeling negative emotions such as guilt, shame and failure.
If I am a good mother I should be able to heal my children.
If I don't give my children what they want then I owe them.
I am not free to relax. I must be hyper-vigilant to keep those I love safe.
Relationships with my children are a constant struggle and filled with pain.

These beliefs could be changed to:

> *My children are responsible for themselves in every way.*
> *If something does not work in my children's lives it is ultimately their choice.*
> *I must detach if my children suffer.*
> *I can be at peace because I am a good mother.*
> *My children can survive and even thrive when they take responsibility for themselves.*
> *My adult children are old souls, powerful and capable.*
> *My children are able to be successful in the world.*
> *I can love my children and feel positive emotions such as love, forgiveness and detachment.*
> *I am a good mother; therefore I allow my children to heal themselves.*
> *If I don't give my children what they want, then they will empower themselves.*
> *I am free to relax. I trust the higher selves of those I love to keep them safe.*
> *Relationships with my children are easy, elegant and filled with joy.*

Become as detached as possible and create your list of beliefs. Sit with each one and ask yourself, *"Is this belief mine?"*

It is important to note that the only one who can truly identify a belief is the person who holds that belief. Others may be able to help, but only *you* can tell if it feels (usually in your gut) like it's yours.

Ready for another clue?

WHAT OTHERS CREATE IS ANOTHER CLUE ABOUT YOUR BELIEFS

Your beliefs will also show up in the lives of others. So ask yourself, what are you creating in the world around you? In the lives of your friends and families? In your community? In society?

Mary might look at what her friends create in *their* relationships. If she sees her friends creating loving, committed relationships, she knows her belief may be that they do exist, but that *she* cannot create one, or is not *worthy* of one.

If she sees men that are untrustworthy liars everywhere she looks, she knows that is likely her belief.

The same with George...if his friends are having an easy time with money, he knows that his beliefs allow money to be created easily...but just not for him.

These subtle differences *do* matter. It is important to find the right belief; otherwise you really aren't changing anything.

WHERE ELSE TO LOOK FOR BELIEFS? WHAT DO YOUR YOUNGER SELVES HAVE TO SAY?

As described previously, our younger selves may have beliefs they picked up long ago—beliefs we, as adults, may be amazed that we still hold.

Remember what the child in the last chapter said about creating wealth: *"You can't have that...don't you remember what Mom said about that?"* Or, *"You are crazy; you can't make things happen like magic!"* Or, they may warn you about the downside of having this dream, *"Once you get the money everyone is going to try and take it away from you...that's what people do."*

The beliefs might be:

> *I cannot create unlimited wealth.*
> *I cannot create my own reality.*
> *Once I create wealth, others will try and take it away.*

It is important to talk with your younger selves. Really listen to them so that you become aware of the beliefs they have given you.

They will tell you what they think. They will share their fears with you. They will tell you why you cannot succeed. Listen. Everything they say is a clue about what they (and you) believe.

MAKING SENSE OF BELIEFS

Beliefs are not hard to change. But it's hard to get people to change beliefs. Why?

Because most people can't accept that they *hold* the very beliefs that need changing, because their conscious mind *doesn't* hold those same beliefs.

Yes, you read that correctly. You can hold two very opposing beliefs at the same time!

I see this a lot when people begin to work on themselves. They very consciously *choose* to believe such things as:

> *The universe is loving.*
> *There is unlimited abundance available to everyone.*
> *I am good enough.*
> *I am unconditionally loved.*
> *It is safe to love.*
> *I create my reality.*

And yet, they have other "selves" that do *not* believe these things. In fact, they believe just the opposite. And those selves have been holding those beliefs for a very long time.

The most deeply held beliefs are creating the reality. And the conscious beliefs keep the deeply held beliefs from being changed. Catch-22 isn't it? What can you do?

First, intend to gently discover the beliefs that are holding you back, and intend to change them with ease and elegance.

You may not want to accept that you hold some of the beliefs that need changing. You may not be proud of them. But remember your reality is a perfect reflection of what you are flowing. Trust *that*. And do what you need to do...be committed to your dream.

BELIEFS: HOW TO CHANGE THEM

There are many methods to change beliefs, from simply saying the new belief over and over, to answering a series of questions to "diffuse" the old belief. I have had amazing success with changing beliefs using variations of the techniques taught by Seth[1] and Lazaris.[2] I love these methods because they address both the conscious and subconscious mind (where the beliefs reside).

The overall components to successfully change a belief are:
1. Word the old belief succinctly but accurately.
2. Choose a new belief and word it similarly to the old belief.
3. Enter the subconscious mind meditatively; destroy the old belief and replace with the new belief.
4. Follow up with the conscious mind.

[1] Seth is an entity who was channeled through Jane Roberts from 1963 to 1984.
[2] For more information visit www.lazaris.com

5. We have just covered the numerous ways to discover your beliefs. The next step is to:

GET CLEAR ON THE WORDING

As I said, it's important to clarify a belief, in order to successfully change it in our subconscious and conscious minds. And it is just as important to word both the new and the old beliefs succinctly and similarly so that the change in the subconscious can be the most elegant and effective possible.

Sometimes it's easy to find clear, precise wording of both the old and new beliefs. Other times you may need to spend some time working with the wording.

Begin with a statement about your reality such as this: *"No matter what I do or how hard I try, whenever I bring a loving relationship into my life it turns out, sooner or later, to bring me pain, and also bring them pain, and after it's over no one is happy and everyone regrets it ever happened."*

The statement may be absolutely true, but long rambling sentences are difficult to change. Why? Because long rambling sentences are not crystal clear. And if they aren't crystal clear to you how could they be crystal clear to your subconscious?

Spend whatever time it takes to think about how you might phrase your belief to be shorter and more succinct, without losing the accuracy. In the example above, I would suggest:

"Love hurts." Or, *"I can't create a loving relationship."* Or, *"(Wo)men always hurt me."*

Then try it on. Say it. It should still have the same or greater emotional tug in your stomach as the first long rambling sentence. And if it feels like a fit, decide what you want the new belief to be.

CHOOSING YOUR NEW BELIEF

The new sentence structure should remain somewhat the same, so that the switching between our subconscious and conscious minds is easier. For instance, *"Love hurts,"* can easily be changed to *"love heals,"* or *"love helps,"* or *"love transcends."*

What should the new beliefs be? Something that makes you excited! Happy! Like you can't wait for them to take root!

Here are some examples from the previous scenarios:

Men are untrustworthy.
Men are trustworthy.

Men always disappoint me.
Men always delight me.

I can't trust my heart when it comes to men.
I can trust my heart when it comes to men.

I can't have a truly loving and committed relationship.
I can have a truly loving and committed relationship.

It's a struggle to create a loving relationship.
It's easy to create a loving relationship.

There are no good men out there.
There are plenty of good men out there (and I only need one).

A good man wouldn't love me.
A good man would cherish me.

I don't deserve.
I do deserve.

Love hurts.
Love expands.

I am not good enough.
I am absolutely good enough.

Money is difficult to create.
Money is easy to create.

Life and money are a struggle. (In this case, break it down into two separate beliefs):

Life is a struggle.
Life is easy.

Money is difficult to create.
Money flows to me easily.

You have to earn money.
You have to receive money.

You must be ever vigilant in creating money.
You will be ever grateful when creating money.

No matter how much I make, there is always just
enough.
No matter how much I spend, there is always more
than enough.

I am not enough.
I am enough.

I am not capable of creating unlimited wealth.
I am more than capable of creating unlimited wealth.

I cannot create my own reality.
I can create my own reality.

Once I create wealth, others will try and take it away.
Once I create wealth, others will be inspired and create it themselves.

THE NEW BELIEF MAY RESULT IN RE-WORDING THE OLD ONE

Sometimes you may discover a negative belief that has been haunting you, such as:

If I am too successful, someone will take it away.

But when you try to write a new belief that says what you want it to say, it just doesn't work, such as:

The more successful I am, the more others are inspired to create success.

The wording in the new belief isn't close enough to the old one. And in order to change a belief easily and successfully, the wording in the old and new belief should be as close as possible. You still need to feel that the old belief is accurate and the new belief is exciting.

What to do? Change the *old* belief. In this example you could change it to:

The more successful I am, the more others will try and take it away from me.

And now it's easy to pair the negative belief with a new belief:

The more successful I am, the more others are inspired to create their own success.

If you read both beliefs aloud (the old and new one), you will see that they both have a similar cadence in the wording. These will be seamlessly changeable in the subconscious mind.

Here is another example. This is a negative belief many people hold about money:

When I am financially abundant I will have to sacrifice my happiness.

But when the positive belief is written, it doesn't really match in wording:

When I am financially abundant, I can be as happy as I decide to be.

Left as written, the belief would probably change in the subconscious mind...but why take that chance? In my experience with changing hundreds of beliefs, those with the same cadence and wording *do* change more easily, quickly and thoroughly.

The reworded old belief says the same thing:

I can't be financially abundant and happy at the same time.

Yet it goes with the new belief perfectly:

> *I can be financially abundant and happy at the same time.*

Discovering and writing new beliefs can be fun work, and a bit challenging in the beginning. Take your time and do it right. The effort will be worth it.

Once you have gotten this far you are almost home. All that remains is the change and follow-up!

THREE LEVELS OF BELIEFS

One of the confusions around beliefs is that they are all the same. They are not.

On one end of the spectrum there are little beliefs that don't have a huge impact on your reality and are easy to change. On the other end there are core beliefs that affect every aspect of your reality and are much more complex to change.

To make belief work easier to understand and work with, I have divided beliefs into three levels with three different methods to change them.

Beliefs

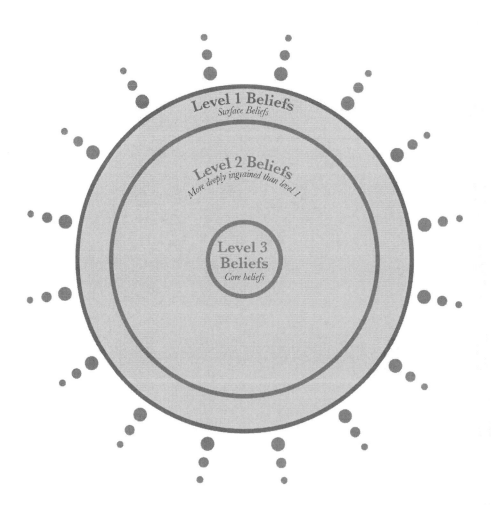

LEVEL ONE BELIEFS

Level one beliefs are the lightest beliefs you have. These are beliefs that are not particularly old, deep or impactful.

A level one belief might be,

> *"It's difficult to learn to roller skate."* Or,

> *"It's hard to meet new people."* Or,

> *"I can't find friends I like."*

Level one beliefs are easy to change. You simply change your thoughts. In this case, you would think (over and over) to yourself:

> *"It's easy to learn to roller skate."* Or,

> *"It's easy to meet new people."* Or,

> *"I can find friends I like."*

If it helps to write them out, by all means do so. But it shouldn't take too long before you feel a shift, a difference, in yourself around this belief. The new belief should start to feel accurate.

What if it doesn't?

Well, maybe it's really a level two belief.

LEVEL TWO BELIEFS

Most of our beliefs (those beliefs that mess with our reality, anyway) are level two beliefs. These beliefs are far more impactful on our reality and far more ingrained in our subconscious than level one beliefs.

Level two beliefs encompass all areas of life. These beliefs were given to us by our parents, our siblings, our grandparents, aunts, uncles, teachers and other authority figures like religious leaders and scout masters. Even society and the media have helped to form our beliefs about the world.

Here are some examples of level two beliefs and what you might change them to:

Possible beliefs about reality:

We really don't create our own realities.
We really do create our own realities.

I do not have the power or ability to create my world.
I do have the power and ability to create my world.

It is hard to create what I want.
It is easy to create what I want.

It is not safe to create all that I want.
It is safe to create all that I want.

I can have the realities I desire after I clear out all my blockages.
I can have the realities I desire now and clear my blockages gradually.

If I am too visible I will be hurt.
I can be visible and I will be loved.

It's hard to change beliefs.
It's easy to change beliefs.

Possible beliefs about money:

You have to earn the money you make.
You can receive the money you make.

If I really live my truth, I'll end up broke.
If I really live my truth, I'll end up wealthy.

Money comes with struggle.
Money comes with ease.

If a lot of money comes easily, it must be illegal.
If a lot of money comes easily, it must be magic.

Making money takes a lot of hard work.
Making money takes a lot of willingness.

When I am rich I won't be able to handle the responsibility.
When I am rich I will be able to handle the responsibility.

When I am rich I won't have time for my spirituality, friends and family.
When I am rich I will have unlimited time for my spirituality, friends and family.

I can't handle success.
I can handle success.

Others are responsible for my success.
I am responsible for my success.

I create just enough money to barely get by.
I create more than enough money for all that I want.

Possible beliefs about work:

I can't make enough money doing what I truly love.
I can make enough money doing what I truly love.

It's a dog-eat-dog world out there.
It's a loving and supportive world out there.

Most entrepreneurs fail, therefore the odds are stacked against me.
Most entrepreneurs succeed, if they know they can create it all.

Success is difficult.
Success is easy.

If I have the work I desire I have to give up things I value.
I can have the work I desire and still have all that I value.

Possible beliefs about relationships:

Great love ends.
Great love endures.

It's not safe to be deeply intimate.
It is safe to be deeply intimate.

I can't have the kind of relationship I want.
I can have the kind of relationship I want.

When I get the kind of relationship I really want, something will happen to destroy it.
When I get the kind of relationship I really want, something will happen to protect it.

When I am in a relationship I will have to keep my
partner at a distance to be safe.
When I am in a relationship I can allow my partner to
be close and still be safe.

It's not OK to have my relationship work smoothly.
It's OK to have my relationship work smoothly.

I can never let my guard down within my relationship.
I can relax and receive sustenance within my
relationship.

If things go too smoothly in my relationship I get ner-
vous and create a problem.
If things go too smoothly in my relationship I feel
happy and create more ease.

I cannot trust men/women.
I can trust some men/women.

Relationships are difficult.
Relationships are easy.

Relationships take huge amounts of energy.
Relationships give huge amounts of energy.

My relationship is never "good enough."
My relationship is always "good and getting better."

I lose myself when I'm in a relationship.
I discover myself when I'm in a relationship.

I give more than I receive in a relationship.
I both give and receive in a relationship.

I am powerless in a relationship.
I am powerful in a relationship.

I can't have lasting love.
I can have lasting love.

I have to do it alone, because there is no one I can really trust but me.
I have tremendous support, and those who support me are trustworthy.

I am never fully safe in a committed relationship.
I am always fully safe in a committed relationship.

I cannot trust the one I love.
I can trust the one I love.

CHANGING A LEVEL TWO BELIEF:

1. Write out or print the old and the new beliefs.

2. Get into a quiet space, and close your eyes. Have your

list of old and new beliefs with you. Call upon your unseen friends (it doesn't matter if you don't know who they are) to assist you. You can say:

"I call on my angels, higher self, guides and others who desire to help me successfully change these beliefs. Gently guide, protect and assist me please, with harm to none."

3. Imagine yourself in a beautiful place in nature. This place is serene, quiet and safe. Then imagine your unseen friends coming to be with you, surrounding you in a bubble of love and light. Take a few moments to close your mental eyes and feel the wonderful love and light. Feel the love, guidance and protection of your unseen friends. When you open your mental eyes you are surrounded in mist. And before you is a grand marble staircase. You, and your unseen friends, begin to walk up this staircase...up, up, up into the clouds.

4. At the very top of this staircase, you will be at the entrance to a city, which represents your subconscious mind. It could be modern or ancient. It could be a city in nature, with natural caves and carvings in the rocks. It could look like anything at all. It may change shape. Whatever it looks like it is perfect for you.

5. The king or queen of this city (your subconscious) will soon come to welcome you. Tell them you want to change your beliefs. They will look to your higher self for permission, and your higher self will nod its consent.

6. Follow the king or queen to the Building of Beliefs. Your higher self will join you. They will take you to the room in this building that holds your level two beliefs. You will enter a gigantic circular room, lined floor to ceiling with filing cabinets. There will be a ladder that slides around the room on a rail, to access the high drawers. You gaze around in amazement.

7. Tell them the first belief you want to change (it's OK to peek at your paper). They will go to a drawer, open it and pull out the belief. It is written out on an 8 x 11 piece of cardstock, plain as day.

8. You take the belief and bring it to a small table in the center of the room. On the table is a big, fat black marker. You take off the cap, and strike through the entire belief. You then rip it into tiny pieces, and place it into a silver bowl lying on the tabletop. Your higher self points a finger, and the belief bursts into flames, quickly extinguishing and leaving nothing, not even ashes, behind.

9. You take a clean, white piece of cardstock from a shelf underneath the table, and with a smaller black marker, write your new belief. Feel your hand shape each letter and say each and every letter in your mind as you write.

10. You hand the new belief to the king/queen and they deftly replace the belief.

11. You repeat this process with every belief you want to change.

12. When you are finished, thank your higher self and the king or queen. They will appreciatively accept your thanks.

13. And when you are ready, open your eyes.

14. Conscious mind follow-up: Write or type out only the new beliefs. Every day, for sixty days, read the new beliefs, with as much excitement and joy as you can muster. (If you skip a day, just add another day at the end.)

That's it! As you see, level two beliefs are a bit more work...but you'll see a lot more change in your life as a result of changing this type of belief.

LEVEL THREE BELIEFS

Level three beliefs are *core* beliefs. These are beliefs that speak to the very nature of *who you are and the world you live in.*

A level three belief might be:

"I don't deserve."

"I am not good enough."

"I don't matter."

"I am not worthy."

"I am flawed."

"I'm not enough."

If you try unsuccessfully to change a belief with a level two process, it's likely to be a level three belief. If you want to be extra sure a belief will change, use the level three approach. It can't hurt.

Level three beliefs are the most important beliefs to change and you will be astounded at how many areas of your life are affected by them. When you change a level three belief, your entire *reality* will shift. That's the upside.

The downside is that it takes more work to change them. But if you follow this procedure with an open heart and mind, and fully feel your emotions along the way, you *can* change a level three belief...believe it or not!

CHANGING A LEVEL THREE BELIEF:

1. Write out why you want to change this belief.

Be specific and really think about how this belief has affected you for your entire life. If for example, you were changing the belief, *"I am not good enough,"* the answer may be something like this:

"I wish to change the belief that I am not good enough because it keeps me stuck in mediocrity. I have always been afraid to try my best. I have a 'why bother' attitude about life and about dreaming bigger dreams. I can't imagine a person of the caliber I want to attract being interested in me.

"This belief has stopped my dreams from manifesting over and over, no matter how close I came to receiving them: Not getting the job at nineteen as the head of maintenance for the stadium; not being accepted to the college I really wanted; losing the internship after college to my best friend, being one of the last three candidates for that job in LA—my dream job— and losing it at the very last minute, etc.

"I purposely hold my dreams small and those I do go for never succeed to the extent they could if I truly believed I was good enough. It has kept me from speaking my truth (what right do I have?). I do not feel worthy of the life I have, let alone a life containing a bigger dream.

"I have passed this belief on to my children, whom I love more than anything. I have judged my friends and relationships as being less than—after all, if they were not losers what were they doing with me? I have stayed in relationships I should have ended. I have been defensive. The list goes on and on."

2. Why *don't* you want to change this belief?

Yes, there is a part of you that *doesn't* want to change the belief. Think about this. What are you afraid of? What could go wrong?

Looking at the same example above, the answer might be:

> *"I don't want to change this belief because I'm afraid it won't work. Then I may as well give up on life because I'll never ever stand a chance of being good enough. I am also a little afraid that it will work. Then I will have no more excuses for not making my life work. That is scary too."*

3. Check in with your child, adolescent and young adult selves.

What do they need to be OK with you changing the belief? Talk to them, individually, and ask them to give you permission to change this belief. Explain to them *why* you want to change it. Ask them what it would take for them to give you the OK. And whatever it is, give it to them. Return to chapter five, if necessary, to review this technique.

4. Write out how your life will change with the new belief.

With the new belief *"I am good enough,"* this might be the answer:

"I will allow my joy and fun and abundance! I will allow more happiness. I will be more secure and kinder and more loving to myself and others. I will be more powerful. I will allow more success! I will be comfortable dreaming bigger dreams and allowing them to manifest. I will be able to make a bigger impact on my world. I will be at peace with speaking my truth."

5. How will your self-concept change with the new belief?

With a belief that "I am good enough," you might see your new self-concept as:

"I am happy, peaceful, content, excited, joyous and fulfilled. I am confident, loving and sure of myself. I am bold in painting my life with joy and people and adventures and experiences. I am at peace, with who I am and who I am becoming."

CHANGING A LEVEL THREE BELIEF IN THE SUBCONSCIOUS MIND:

(Note: steps 1-4 are identical to changing a level two belief.)

1. Write out or print out the old and the new beliefs.

2. Get into a quiet space, and close your eyes. Have your list of old and new beliefs with you. Call upon your unseen

friends (it doesn't matter if you don't know who they are) to assist you. You can say:

"I call on my angels, higher self, guides and others who desire to help me successfully change these beliefs. Gently guide, protect and assist me please, with harm to none."

3. Imagine you are in a beautiful place in nature. This place is serene, quiet and safe. Then imagine your unseen friends coming to be with you, surrounding you in a bubble of love and light. Take a few moments to close your mental eyes and feel the wonderful love and light. Feel the love, guidance and protection of your unseen friends. When you open your mental eyes you are surrounded in mist. And before you is a grand marble staircase. You, and your unseen friends, begin to walk up this staircase...up, up, up into the clouds.

4. At the very top of this staircase, you will be at the entrance to a city, which represents your subconscious mind. It could be modern or ancient. It could be a city in nature, with natural caves and carvings in the rocks. It could look like anything at all. It may change shape. Whatever it looks like it is perfect for you.

5. The king or queen of this city (your subconscious) will soon come to welcome you. Tell them you want to change your beliefs. They will look to your higher self for permission, and your higher self will nod its consent. "Are you SURE, they will ask?" Your higher self will look at you, and back at the king/queen and say, *"Yes, it is time."*

6. Follow the king or queen to the Building of Beliefs. Your higher self will join you. They will take you to the room that holds your level three beliefs. They press a secret button—you cannot tell exactly how—and an entire section of cabinets opens up to reveal a secret door.

7. The king/queen goes through the doorway and beckons you to follow. You and your higher self do follow, but you barely catch a glimpse of them as they head down a hallway, and then turn a corner. They twist through long passageways, this way and that. Finally they enter an elevator and you follow, barely making it in before the doors close. The elevator goes up, over, down, then down, over and up...over and over. You have entirely lost track of where you are. The doors open, and the king/queen/ leads you to a door marked, "Core Beliefs: Do Not Enter."

8. They unlock the door and allow you to enter. It is a small room. A table sits in the middle of it and on the table is a thin book marked, "My Core Beliefs." *"Now,"* the king/ queen says, *"Tell me the belief you want to change."*

9. Tell them the belief you want to change. They open the book to exactly that belief.

10. Picking up the thick black marker, you cross out the belief obliterating every word. You rip the page neatly out of the book and tear it into tiny shreds. Your higher self looks at you and asks, *"Are you certain? This will change everything."*

You nod your head. And your higher self points its finger and the belief bursts into flames, leaving nothing behind.

11. You look down at a clean white page in the book, pick up a thin black marker and begin to write your new belief, saying each and every letter in your mind as you write.

12. You put down the marker and close the book.

13. Your higher self and your subconscious mind are grinning. You grin back, thanking them with your eyes. You say your goodbyes, close your mental eyes and allow yourself to be back where you started...but you are different.

14. Open your eyes.

15. Conscious mind follow up: Write or type out the new belief. Every day, for ninety days, read the new belief twice a day, with as much excitement and joy as you can muster. (If you skip a day, just add another day at the end.)

BELIEF WORK—MORE POWERFUL THAN YOU CAN IMAGINE

I have changed hundreds of beliefs in my lifetime. And every single time, it doesn't seem like anything is happening at first. That is the mystery around changing beliefs. Since they seem to be so much a part of "how life is" you don't see them as changeable.

And after you change them, it seems that the new belief is "how life is"—and it's as though it's *always* been that way, and nothing has really changed. But then, you watch, amazed as your life changes before your very eyes, *if you continue following The Map.*

Remember belief work is still only *stopping* the negative flow of energy. You still need to flow energy to what you *do* want. In the next chapter, you will learn precisely how to do that.

LIFE-ALTERING TAKE AWAYS

Read these slowly. Meditate on them or sit and contemplate them. Let them in. Let them change you.

+ Beliefs are thoughts and feelings that are *wired* into your system. These are thoughts and feelings that are so solid you take them as *absolute truth*. And you emit that energy, which in turn creates your reality, one hundred percent of the time.

+ When you change your beliefs you literally change your world. Your success. Your finances. Your health. Your relationships. *Everything* changes.

+ It will take some detective work to uncover the beliefs that are creating what you *don't* want. Where do you begin? You begin by *paying attention*. You pay attention to:

> What you think.
> What you feel.
> What you say.
> What you do.
> What you create.

+ The absolute *best* way of discovering your beliefs is to look at what you have *already created*. You may deceive yourself—or be unconscious of the truth—but your reality *never* lies. It reflects as clear as day what you really, deep down, truly *believe*.

✦ There are three critical questions to ask yourself when you are seeking to uncover your beliefs:
1. What do I want to create?
2. What have I created?
3. What would someone have to believe to have created this?

✦ The overall components to successfully change a belief are:
1. Word the old belief succinctly but accurately.
2. Choose a new belief and word it similarly to the old belief.
3. Enter the subconscious mind meditatively; destroy the old belief and replace with the new belief.
4. Follow up with the conscious mind.

YOUR NEXT STEPS

☐ Do you have any old emotional baggage from a disappointment, a betrayal or a hurt that you need to let go of? Write a "hate" letter to yourself, God or another person. Then forgive both yourself and others.

☐ Consider your work with your child, adolescent and young adult selves in the previous chapter. Do you have any beliefs you need to change about your ability to successfully create a life you love? These are likely level two beliefs. Change them now.

☐ Think about the core (level three) beliefs listed below:

> *"I don't deserve."*
> *"I am not good enough."*
> *"I don't matter."*
> *"I am not worthy."*
> *"I am flawed."*
> *"I'm not enough."*

Do you hold any of these beliefs? If so, change them.

Desire

Energy

You create your own reality. You are a divine spark of consciousness - a part of God, a part of Goddess, a part of everything.

SEVEN

TECHNIQUES TO INCREASE THE FLOW

"Expressing feelings is linked directly with creation...
In this ability *to tap the sources of feeling and
imagination lies the secret of abundance."*

—ANAIS NIN

Techniques make things happen in the world of conscious creation. They focus that flow of energy in a laser-like way and speed the manifestation process way up. There are neither good nor bad techniques, only effective or ineffective techniques *for you*.

Use the techniques that make you feel good and powerful and don't use the techniques that don't. If you can find techniques that are fun, even better!

But don't forget it isn't the technique that makes the magic happen, it is you. Here are a few powerful techniques for you to play with:

IGNITING INTENTIONS TECHNIQUE

You have your intentions written out, right?

Igniting Intentions is a technique to light them on fire (metaphorically, folks) and notify all the aspects of you and the world at large, that you are ready to see them through to manifestation!

This technique is a way to put attention on, and flow energy to, everything on your list of intentions.

Every morning, and every evening, read your intentions (out loud if it is comfortable to do so).

What? You don't have time? Excuse me??

The creation of your world should be your top priority. Kids? Put 'em in the intentions. Job? It too. Spouse? Of course he or she should be there.

Everything in your world should be in your intentions. Since you are creating everything anyway, you may as well create everything the way you desire it.

If your intentions are *not* the most important thing in your life, you don't understand the way your universe works.

So, read your intentions (ideally) each morning and every evening before bed. With excitement! With joy! With love and gratitude because the more you can *feel* these states of emotion the more quickly your intentions will manifest in your world!

A DAY IN THE DAY OF THE DREAM TECHNIQUE

A Day in the Day of the Dream technique is to live (emotionally) a day in the life of the person you are becoming. You basically pretend that you *already* are that person. This does not mean you max out your credit cards because you want to become a millionaire.

It does mean feeling as though you have all the money in the world.

It takes a pretty good imagination, but once you start this technique, let me warn you, it may become addictive. And if you do it correctly, it will eventually seem that this *is* you. And after that, it won't be long before your world will deliver the manifestations that you have created in your "feels oh so real" playacting.

So how might it "play" out? Like this:

Her dream is to become an internationally known, award-winning writer who is independently wealthy and has a fabulous relationship with a man she adores. She has won the Nobel Peace Prize and has single-handedly helped scores of people become empowered, fulfilled and happy. Her health and vitality continue to improve; the older she becomes the younger she feels. And every single area of her life is working.

So **A Day in the Day of the Dream** might look like this:

She wakes up, and imagines the love of her life lying next to her. Quietly, so not to wake him, she gets out of bed and gives thanks for the glorious day ahead of her. She thinks of how wonderful it feels to love and to be loved, and as she brushes her teeth, she thinks about kissing him awake.

(Now mind you, there is no one in her bed—in case you were wondering. And even if there *were* a man in her bed, and she wanted greater love, respect and caring in her current relationship, feeling those emotions would draw that reality to her.)

She patters into the kitchen to put on some coffee. How would a Nobel Prize winner make and drink coffee? Very slowly while thinking up new things to write about, she decides. And she does just that. As she sits in contemplation, she starts to worry about the bills coming due. She shoves those thoughts away, bound and determined to spend this day emotionally as if she had her dream. What does a person who has more than enough money for everything she ever wanted think about?

Someone who doesn't have to think about money doesn't think about money, she decides. Instead she thinks about the impact her work might have. And she becomes excited about that.

Later she drives to the supermarket to pick up some groceries, and as she gets into her car, she imagines the smell of the new leather interior of the sporty foreign car she dreams of. Driving carefully, as she would if she possessed a car worth ten times her current one, she looks for a wide parking space that would honor the beauty of her dream vehicle. And she parks there.

As she shops she imagines she does this, not because she doesn't have people to do it for her in her dream, but to stay connected to the earth. She chooses her fruits and vegetables with a sense of grace and dignity...knowing that her work has impacted millions of people and this, communing with the bounty of the earth, is her reward.

Driving home, she realizes that if she already had all the things she has dreamed about, she would be calmer. More focused. At peace. So she settles into a peaceful, happy state of being, imagining that she has every reason to be peaceful and happy. Tomorrow I can go back to worrying about what I don't have, she thinks...or maybe not.

As she makes dinner, she tries worldwide success on for size. Would I be able to go to the store without people recognizing me, she wonders? Would being famous, even in a small arena, destroy my anonymity and my ability to be out in public without harassment? And then she remembers that if she can create her success, she can create the consequences of that success as well.

Sometimes people will recognize me, and that's OK, she thinks, for I will create them to be respectful and kind. They will only want to share the impact my words have had on them...and that is a good thing.

As she settles into bed at the end of the day, she imagines deep love coming from the man in bed with her, his arms wrapped tightly around her, and she falls asleep with love in her heart and mind.

A Day in the Day of the Dream technique can be fun. It will give you a chance to really try on the image of who you want to become, and it may point out some beliefs or thoughts that need to change.

MAKE THE MOVIE REAL TECHNIQUE

This is an easy, fun and powerful technique. You simply close your eyes and imagine walking up to a movie theatre...the old fashioned kind with a marquee outside and a stage within. As you look up to the marquee, you see your name in lights! The marquee announces: "_____'s Life in Five Years!"

Intrigued, you excitedly head in...the theatre is empty and you sit in the front row. The lights dim, the curtains open, and the movie begins. You see yourself, the "you" you want to become, with the life you desire on the screen. Perhaps an average day for you five years from now, or perhaps a special day—receiving an award, a wedding, moving into a new house, on vacation, etc.

You watch this "you" for a while, and at some point, it just looks so real, so three-dimensional, you climb onto the stage and step into that life. Up close, you observe this you.

And then, because "you" are having so much fun, you step into your future body. And suddenly you *are* the future "you." Hang out there for a while. Have fun with it. Really feel the emotions, and allow yourself to *be* that future you. And when you are ready, close your mental eyes and feel yourself back in the here and now.

And if you feel a little different, that is a good thing. This will change you. Little by little, bit by bit. Embrace the change.

GRATEFUL FOR "NOW AND THEN" TECHNIQUE

Gratitude is an amazing force. And this is an amazing technique. (And easy too!)

Start by opening a new document in your computer, or a new page in your creation journal. Write ten things you feel grateful for today. Then file it under that date in your computer.

Now write ten things you will be grateful for at some point in the future. It could be a year, a week, or a month. Don't go too far out though. As you write, really let in the joy of what you want to experience, as if it has already happened.

That's it. Do this every day, week or month. And when that future date rolls around, open the document. See how you did!

This exercise only needs to take ten or fifteen minutes. What is more important than your life? Anything? Wake up. Make time.

Here are mine from 2/22/12:

Ten Now:

1. I am grateful for my wonderful husband, whose love brings me great joy.
2. I am grateful for the beautiful ocean, which I gaze at as I write this.
3. I am grateful for the ability to spend good chunks of time in the islands, where I can focus on my writing in a gorgeous, serene and inspirational atmosphere.
4. I am grateful for the beauty this planet has to offer.
5. I am grateful for my unseen friends, who help me every step of the way.
6. I am grateful for the cat I brought to live in the islands, and for the chance to know him better.
7. I am grateful for the love I feel from my family and friends.

8. I am grateful for the sun, and for the water.
9. I am grateful for my prosperity and abundance. It is wonderful to feel so free financially.
10. I am grateful for my ability to write, for it brings me great joy.

Ten Then (One year from now):

1. I am grateful for my health and my body. I love my body and am grateful for its continued "youthening," suppleness and vitality.
2. I am extremely grateful for my husband and his love. I feel our relationship deepening continually and growing exponentially.
3. I am grateful that my real estate companies have become so easy, elegant and profitable. I am always excited to invest in new homes, feel their energies and send lots of sparkling light to make them beautiful for the perfect tenant. This has become a wonderful, love and light-filled hobby.
4. I am grateful that my work has taken off so beautifully. My first book has become an award-winning success and my second promises to be wildly successful also.
5. I am grateful that my readers/students are manifesting such stupendous miracles and magic in their lives. It feels so wonderful to assist them in finding their power and using it to create their dreams.
6. I am grateful that my relationships are where I always dreamed they would be...deep and fulfilling bonds

with my friends and family that provide me with great satisfaction and love.

7. I am grateful for the beauty that surrounds me, in my homes, in my travels, and on this planet.

8. I am extremely grateful for the professional help I've received from mentors across the globe. People whose guidance and expertise have been truly miraculous in helping me navigate the international publishing world.

9. I am grateful for my art progressing so magically...the sculpting and painting I've always dreamed of doing is now a reality!

10. I am grateful for the mystery and magic of creativity. I love, love, love that and have so much fun pulling from places deep inside me!

I was in awe, when I wrote this, at how profound and uplifting it felt. I was grateful for the "Now" list, but even more gratitude poured out of me for the "Ten Then." Try it. Have fun. Don't forget to look back when "then" comes around to see what a fabulous creator you have become!

FLOW AND LET GO...

Flowing energy, if done correctly, is where the magic really happens. You have checked to make sure that you are not stopping the flow, and you then did some powerful techniques to flow energy...now what?

Now, you let go.

What? I want to know the next step...I want to keep going. What do I do next?

We will get to that. I promise. Right now, just *be*. Be OK in the knowing that you have done what it takes, and now the universe will take over and deliver your dream.

But wait, I don't want to let go...maybe I should do more techniques? Tell me what to do next!

Nothing. You do nothing. You have already done enough...in this moment. The energy of letting go and trusting that you will receive the essence of your desire is an important one.

Essence? What do you mean essence? I ordered money!

Letting go means knowing you will *get* what you want. And ultimately, you *don't* want money.

Wait, yes I do!

No, you don't. You want what money can give you.

Yeah, well, I guess.

You want freedom to go places and experience the things you want to experience.

True.

And you want safety, security, beauty, pleasure and joy.

That is absolutely true.

And what if it were delivered to you...without money?

What? How?

You are trying to control the universe again. It is not *yours* to figure out how. It is yours to order the essence of your deepest desires. And you do that by feeling the beautiful, inspiring, rich and positive emotions of having the thing(s) you want... and then letting go.

The universe knows the most elegant way to bring you what you want. To try and control it will only add the energies of doubt, impatience, distrust and lack.

Your energy should be telling the universe, *"I already have my dream."*

Why on earth would you be trying to control receiving what you already have? It never works.

Besides, the universe is set up for this. It delivers what you flow one hundred percent of the time. Guaranteed. Better than FedEx. There is no way you can beat that.

So I do one technique and let go and that's it?

No. You do as many techniques as it feels fun and powerful to do. But you don't let yourself slip into desperation or impatience.

Desperation energy tells the universe, *"I'm afraid I won't get what I want so I have to somehow hedge my bets by doing technique after technique after technique."*

Impatience energy tells the universe, *"I don't have what I want,"* when you *want* to tell the universe, *"I already have what I want."*

"Flow and let go" means you do a technique (or as many as feels fun), and you let go. The next time it feels like fun to do a technique, do it. But then let go. Be patient. Give the universe a chance to do its job.

THE SECRET TO "LETTING GO"

Learning to let go when you *really* want something can be tough. But there *is* something you can develop to allow this piece to be easier—in fact, it will allow the whole process to be easier. What is it?

Trust.

Now I know, trust is a bit of a Catch-22. How can you trust in something you've seldom (or never) done before?

Well, let's take a look at it. What you're really asking yourself to do is:

Trust you will receive what you want. And...

Trust you will be OK until you get what you want.

When we are talking about issues of survival, this can be especially challenging. It becomes tempting to slide back into scarcity, lack and feeling like a victim. What can you do?

You begin by trusting *your own sense of inner knowing* about what is true. But there may be some aspects of you that do not hold such a knowing. In fact, they (your child and adolescent selves) probably hold quite opposite beliefs.

It will help you to increase your trust, if you change these beliefs, *now*, rather than years from now:

Reality is real.
Change it to: *Reality is an illusion.*

I don't create my entire reality.
Change it to: *I do create my entire reality.*

Life is a struggle.
Change it to: *Life is a gift.*

I cannot trust myself.
Change it to: *I can* trust *myself.*

After you've changed any unsupportive beliefs, it's time to "practice" letting go. How do you do that? By understanding what it looks like to *not* let go.

You are holding on too tightly if you:

Are concerned that it *hasn't* manifested yet.

Continually wonder when it *will* manifest.

Wonder if it *has* manifested and what you've received is all you'll get.

Are afraid it *won't* manifest at all (or won't manifest by a certain time).

Letting go means letting the universe handle the details of the manifestation and trusting it will happen. It can help you to train yourself to respond to the above fears in a way that puts your anxieties to rest. Such as:

"Although my dream has not yet found its way to my reality, I know in my heart it is on its way. I have done the techniques, cleared the beliefs, and it's just a matter of time now."

"I do not need to wonder when my dream will manifest, because if I feel how it will feel when I have it, it's as good as manifested anyway. Let me practice that now..."

"I am safe. I am protected. I am loved by the universe, myself and many unseen friends. Instead of feeling fear right now, I now choose to feel excitement about what I am creating!"

With some practice and some successes under your belt, this will get easier and easier. I promise.

HOW I LEARNED TO LET GO (IN MORE WAYS THAN ONE)

In the realm of relationships more than in any other arena we have a tendency to try to control others and the outcome. And I was no exception to that rule. One of the toughest lessons for me was in letting go and trusting I would (eventually) get what I wanted in a loving partnership.

I had been working at creating a relationship since I was divorced from my first husband over a dozen years prior. Men would come and go in my life, but none of them lived up to my vision. This was before I discovered the power of intentions, but I still wrote out my desire:

My desire in a relationship:

I desire and am attracting a man who is strong, power-
ful and successful in his own right. He is spiritual as
well as metaphysical—a true magician. He is compas-
sionate, loving and whole. He shares a similar sense
of humor and we connect on mental, spiritual, emo-
tional and physical levels. There is an inherent safety in
my relationship with him. He is emotionally and physi-
cally available. He is willing and capable of continuing
to stretch further and further into the depths of love.

We share a similar passion...for each other, for life and
for making the world a better place. He is loyal, com-
mitted, romantic and sensual. We love nothing more
than to bring each other happiness and joy. He is hon-
est with me and intensely honest with himself. He is
willing to look at his stuff and call me (gently and lov-
ingly) on mine. He is committed to his growth.

We have so much fun when we are together! Laughter
is abundant and we deeply enjoy each other's com-
pany. We have our independent lives and projects but
we also have special projects we work on together.
The synergy of our magic together creates spectacu-
lar results that amaze even us.

I feel tremendously loved and valued by him. He
makes our relationship a priority in his life, as do I,
although we both have a full and rich life outside of

our union. He and I share similar tastes in music, art, entertainment, physical activities and how to spend our time together. He is supportive and champions me and my work, as I do him and his.

We are completely compatible and our lives seem "charmed" to everyone, including us, as we flow together through our days. Synchronicities happen over and over that support us in our relationship and commitment to each other. When we disagree, we are able to work/talk/feel through it with respect and compassion for each other.

We genuinely love and enjoy each other's family and friends. We are uncannily drawn to the same places in the world, and happily cohabitate. We are similar in the important aspects, such as values, ideals, commitments, and complement each other in other areas so that together we form a synergy of love and joy.

It is a gift, each and every time I think of him, am near him or spend time with him. I want everyone to know him because he is so wonderful. He brings me joy beyond my wildest dreams. I love him so. And loving him makes me more. He is my gift from God and the Goddess.

I did some techniques here and there. And I **let it go.** I focused on my work and moving into my new home in nearby Boulder.

I met Richard on a blind date. While I wouldn't call it love at first sight, we fell in love soon afterward. In many ways it was idyllic. He swept me off my proverbial feet and introduced me to a lifestyle I'd never even dreamed of.

Our second date was a whirlwind tour of his palatial ranch, his airplane hangar filled with jets of all sizes and a construction site where his new restaurant was being built. Within weeks we were jetting off to the Bahamas, staying on his sailboat and taking his sea-plane to deserted islands, where we snorkeled, swam and picnicked.

And the moment he took my head in his hands and looked deep into my eyes as I floated in the warm, turquoise blue water…I fell in love. We became engaged just two months after we met. *"This is what I asked for,"* I thought. *"Thank you!"*

Although the love was deep, our relationship was plagued with difficulties from the start. We were aligned in many very important ways, such as our values, our beliefs and our desire to be of service, yet we were quite opposite in the more earthly aspects of life.

He was social, outgoing, very active physically and loved to be around people—the more the merrier. I loved my solitude, chose long slow walks and meditation over more active sports, and preferred intimate one-on-ones rather than large soirées. And even *those* differences weren't deal breakers.

Maybe we believed the love was too good to be true. Maybe we focused too much on what *wasn't* right instead of what was. We fought often and passionately, but I never stopped believing we could make it work. He, however, did. He broke it off three times in a row. And after the third time, I knew it was over.

I had thought I had created "the one" and I was deeply disappointed. But I wasn't through trying. I was more determined than ever to create the relationship I longed for. I **let go** of Richard and trusted that the universe had a better match for me.

I forgave myself. I went back to the drawing board and revisited my beliefs about men, love and relationships. I took ownership for *my* part in the breakup. After all, I was creating it too. And I had an epiphany...I realized I had been so busy trying to *protect* the relationship by controlling my partner that I squeezed much of the joy out of the union.

Undaunted, I went on another blind date and met John. We hit it off and I (again) became engaged within two months. *"Richard must have prepared me for John,"* I thought. *"John is* 'the one!'" John and I were more alike in some ways. He was even more of an introvert than I am! And he was a writer with a spiritual message.

"Hurray! I finally did it," I thought.

I discovered four months later that although we had similar temperaments we had very *dissimilar* values. He lied to me about not one but *three* very important issues. I felt betrayed and angry. I broke off the engagement and wrote a very nasty hate letter to release my anger (and burned it after I made it as strong as I could).

Back to the drawing board one more time. Obviously I still had some negative beliefs about men and relationships. I changed them. And I visited a psychic—a gift from one of my workshop attendees. She "saw" me in a wonderful relationship. "*Oh no,*" I said, "*I am not in one and right now don't plan to be in one for a while.*" I explained what had happened during the prior year.

It was then that she gave me some remarkable advice. "*These two men and every man you've ever dated have been a gift to you. They have readied you for the relationship you dream of. But unless you* **let them go with love and gratitude** *you will never create the one you really want.*"

How right she was. I had been seeing all the "failed" relationships as, well, failures. But they weren't failures. They were successes. Each and every one had something for me to be grateful for. I learned, I grew and I loved, to the best of my ability at the time.

And because I viewed my past relationships as failures, I viewed myself as a "failure in relationships." Ouch. No wonder I wasn't creating what I wanted.

I bought a journal. I went back to every relationship I ever had, from age thirteen through the present. And I wrote about what was good about that person and the relationship. And then, I blessed them all, and *let them go*.

Of course I continued to dream and flow energy towards the relationship I wanted.

When Richard continued to contact me, I was polite but dismissive. I just didn't think he had what it took to work through the issues that a long term commitment brings up. I thought we could be friends, though, and I agreed to an occasional lunch or dinner.

A year after our break up, I sat in a restaurant with him, listening to him talk about something he was passionate about. And it hit me. I still loved him. Deeply.

I didn't feel that I could show my love because it would give him the wrong idea. We had already proven that a romantic relationship just wouldn't work. And I wasn't being a good friend because I was holding back my true feelings. I'd have to give up the friendship. It seemed like a "lose-lose" scenario and I needed to cut the ties and move on.

That's when I talked with one of my guides. She said, *"Why not give Richard a chance? You have to practice being your authentic self in a relationship anyway. Practice on him. And who knows…he may be able to step into the relationship you truly desire."*

Wait. I had let go of Richard to make room for John. And I had let go of John to make room for...Richard?

What I did then was to **truly let go.** I let go of any expectation of "who" was going to show up at all. I let go of what it had to "look like." I let go of the past...of the disappointments *and* of the triumphs. I let go of all judgments about who Richard was or wasn't.

I just showed up and tried to be as authentic, loving and conscious as possible. And an amazing thing happened. As I allowed *him* to be free of the past, I also allowed him to be *different* in our present.

We fell in love, all over again. And we were married, just a few months later. And while it's not perfect (*nothing* is *ever* perfect, folks), it *is* the relationship I have always dreamed of. And in it, I *do* feel how I always wanted to feel. Loved. Loving. Joyful. Safe. And secure.

LIFE-ALTERING TAKE AWAYS

Read these slowly. Meditate on them or sit and contemplate them. Let them in. Let them change you.

+ Techniques *make things happen* in the world of conscious creation. They focus that flow of energy in a laser-like way and speed the manifestation process *way* up. There are neither good nor bad techniques, only effective or ineffective techniques *for you.*

+ Letting go means letting the universe handle the details of the manifestation and trusting it *is going to* happen. Although this may always present somewhat of a challenge, it *will* get easier.

YOUR NEXT STEPS

☐ Pick an area of your life that you would like to see change. Journal about your past in that area (career, money, relationships, etc.), listing the major happenings (jobs, financial history, partners, etc.) and write about what was good about them and what you learned. Then let them go with love.

☐ Choose one of these techniques:

   A Day in the Day of the Dream
   Make the Movie Real
   Grateful for "Now and Then"

   Do it right now. *Practice makes realities.*

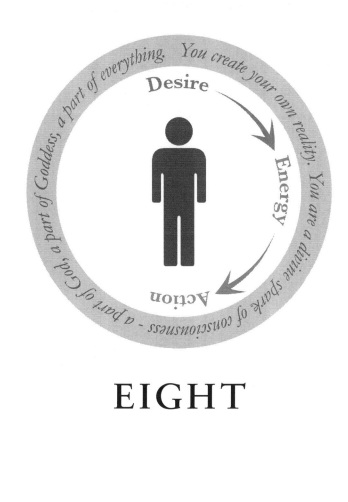

EIGHT

ACTION: ACCELERATING THE PROCESS

"Your thoughts are powerful creators, and your words are even more powerful than your thoughts, but your actions are more powerful than your words or your thoughts."

—ABRAHAM

If you have a dream and are not acting on it I say you have a fantasy, not a dream. And hey, that's cool. Fantasies are fun.

But they are also frivolous. And they seldom, if ever, manifest in reality.

All I ask is—don't fool yourself. And don't give this Universe of Free Will a bad name by pretending you don't create it all because your "dream" didn't happen.

To have a dream without action gives the universe conflicting messages. On one hand, you say you want this dream, on the other, you don't really expect it to happen.

What! Of course I expect it to happen!

If you did, my friend, you would be taking action—showing the universe you *are* serious about this dream and fully expect its manifestation.

HOLD ON...

I'm not talking about blind action. If your dream is to move to Bali, I am not talking about getting on a bus today despite not having the money to make it further than Poughkeepsie.

I am talking about taking small, definitive steps towards that dream. For example, you could:

Buy a book on Bali.

Join an online forum of expats who now live in Bali.

Plan an exploratory trip to Bali.

Make plans about what you will take, how much that will cost, and pare down your belongings now.

Wait, I don't want to begin getting rid of things—what if I never move there?

My friend, if you aren't sure enough that you want to move to Bali to begin to get rid of things in preparation to go, you should *not* be intending to move to Bali!

Instead, your intentions might be something like this:

> *I intend to become clear on where I want to live.*
> *I intend to live in a place that is beautiful, warm, sensuous, loving, spiritual and exciting.*
> *I intend to have fun adventures in my life.*
> *I intend to try out various places to live (including Bali) in the next few years in an easy, elegant, flowing and freeing fashion.*

Notice the new intentions do not preclude Bali, but they expand into a much wider range of possibilities.

These possibilities could manifest as a job with international travel (adventure) and a home base in sunny California or Florida (beautiful and warm) in a community so loving and connected (sensuous and spiritual) that you are filled with all of the qualities you desire and more. You meet the love of your life there (loving) and suddenly you can't imagine living anywhere else (clarity!).

Now maybe you didn't know you weren't that clear about moving to Bali until it came time to sell off some of your stuff...and it doesn't really matter. What does matter is that when you start taking action, if you are paying attention, you *do* become clearer.

But more than that, taking action speaks volumes to your subconscious mind. Action solidifies your intention and strengthens your flow of energy towards that dream. *Action is part of creation.*

BUT WHAT IF YOU DON'T FEEL LIKE TAKING ACTION?

I understand not wanting to take action—I've been there myself many times. But...

Taking action is part of creating anything.

"Wait," you might say, *"if I can create anything, can't I create things just falling into my lap without taking any action at all?"*

Very clever. Although theoretically, yes, you could sit back and do nothing and expect things to fall into your lap, it's just not going to work as well. Why?

Three reasons:

1. **Action is a proving ground.** If you have clarified the desire and then flowed positive energy to the desire, taking action should feel great. If it doesn't, that's a clue to go back to understand *why*. If taking action doesn't feel good, or you aren't motivated to take action, something is wrong and needs tending to.

2. **Action intensifies the energies and speeds up the manifestation.** Positive emotion (such as excitement, happiness, freedom, love) directed towards a thought—your job, relationship or finances—with supporting beliefs (i.e. I believe I can have this, deserve it, can create it, etc.) *will* create your reality. If you felt joyous about what you wanted and believed you could have it, you would *want* to get out there and begin doing it, preparing for it, taking steps towards it, etc. Those actions create more positive energy, which allows your reality to shift, creating what you want sooner!

3. **Action is (or should be) part of the *fun*.** The old adage, *"it's not about the destination it's about the journey,"* is a critically important concept in manifesting your dreams. It's the energy of the fun, excitement

and fulfillment you feel along the way that draws to you the reality you desire. Action helps. You know you are on the right path when the journey towards your dreams is a blast, and that includes the action steps!

SO WHAT'S GOING ON IF YOU DON'T FEEL LIKE TAKING ACTION?

One of three things is likely going on:

1. Either you don't really *want* what you say you want, or

2. You don't believe you can *have* what you want, or

3. You've lost touch with the *essence* of your desire.

If you really want what you say you want, if you believe you can have it, and if you've held tightly to the essence of your dream, *nothing* would be able to stop you from taking action. You would be so excited, so juiced, so enthralled with getting this thing and expecting it to show up that you would be preparing for it every chance you got.

An example from my life:

> *When I was in the midst of manifesting a loving partnership, I began thinking about the partner I intended to attract. I thought about what it would be like when he stayed over, or even moved into my*

home. I imagined what I would feel like when he showed up—the safety, security, love, fun, joy, trust and gratitude. I was so excited!

The action: I cleaned out and reorganized my closet. I bought a dresser for him. I bought hangers. I added some Feng Shui touches to the bedroom.

The result: within a couple of months he came into my life.

But if you aren't excited, if you don't want to take action, look deeper at why not.

MAYBE IT ISN'T *REALLY* WHAT YOU WANT

I know someone who *said* he wanted to be a doctor. But he hated the idea of spending years and years in medical school.

When he looked deeper into his motivation, he realized he didn't really *want* to be a doctor after all. He was *really* after money and prestige.

Upon further self-examination, he realized he wanted the prestige to prove to others that he was *valuable*.

He worked at healing his self-perception, changing the belief that he wasn't valuable without the degree and eventually he realized the money flows where there is most excitement and passion (if you believe it can). He discovered a career he loved and became quite wealthy as a result.

And if you look at whether you really have the desire, and you do, but you are still not excited enough to act, then:

MAYBE YOU DON'T BELIEVE YOU CAN CREATE IT

One of the biggest reasons people don't feel like taking action is that they don't, on a subconscious level, *really* believe anything will come of it. Oh, they *want* to believe it. But they don't.

And they don't want to admit that to themselves because the disappointment would be too much to handle. Better to hold onto the fantasy, even if it never manifests, than to admit that it never will.

As we know, beliefs can be changed. And being brutally honest with yourself is the only way to discover what holds you back. So if you're just not feeling inspired to act, ask yourself... *"Do you really believe you can create it?"*

If the answer is, *"Not really,"*...find that belief and change it!

You can create anything you can imagine...one step at a time. But if you get to the action step, and you really want the thing you are creating and you honestly believe it is possible...and yet you still aren't motivated to move...

MAYBE YOU'VE LOST TOUCH
WITH THE ESSENCE

The essence is the heart of the dream. It is what makes the dream manifest and it is the reason you desire it. The essence is the state of being you want to experience after you have received the dream—the excitement, the joy, the love, the creativity, the fun, the abundance, etc.

Remembering the essence or feeling state, can reignite the dream and inspire action. Think about the essence your dream will give you. Write down and feel those feelings as often as you can. Also doing any of the techniques in chapter seven will help you to get back in touch with the essence. You will then be delightfully inspired to "act!"

Also, know *why* you are taking action

The entire world can be yours, *is* yours, for the taking. But you will not allow yourself to receive it if you are not OK with the reason(s) you are creating it.

For example, what if one of your motivations for creating wealth is to feel better than other people? Even though the universe doesn't care what your motivation is, if you (or some part of you) feel that it is not OK you won't allow it.

So along with that idea, know *why* you are taking action. If it is merely to acquire *things*, and this is a spiritual lifetime for you, you may not allow yourself to succeed.

Wait, I thought we could have anything! Just for the asking?

You can. The universe will never deny you.

You may deny you though.

The way you can tell if you are in alignment with a motivation on all levels, and the way you can tell if the action has power behind it, is this: does it bring you joy?

A simple and profound question. Does the action bring you joy?

If it does, you can assume you are on the right track.

If it does not, take another look at your dreams, your beliefs and your motivation. And rework them until the action you take towards your dreams *does* bring you joy, excitement and fulfillment.

HOW DO YOU KNOW
WHAT ACTION TO TAKE?

OK. You know that taking action is an important step in manifesting your desires. But you are confused as to where to begin, right?

Don't worry. This happens to everyone at one point or another. The first and most important thing to ask when considering what action to take is this: what most excites you?

Do not—repeat—do not take action just to take action. Do not take action to "prove" to yourself or anyone else that you believe in your dream. Do not take action if you feel like it's your duty or obligation or because you think you should. Those types of actions will stop your dream from coming!

What? The "wrong" action can stop my dream?

Yes! Taking action with an underlying feeling of martyrdom, desperation or a need to "earn" your reality will stop your dream! And come on now, you've come so far, with setting those intentions and flowing energy towards your desire...you owe it to yourself and your future self to get this step right.

And if the motivation to act out of excitement isn't readily available to you, that's OK. It may just take a little finessing. Begin by slowing down. Take some time, get away from email, phone, family and friends, and just *be* with yourself and your dream.

And think about what you want. Feel how it will feel when you get it. Imagine for a moment, that you could not fail. No way. No how. Success was guaranteed. Stay focused now; don't let your mind wander.

So feeling the excitement and joy of having this thing you want, and knowing that you *do* want to do something—you're just not quite sure what it is, ask yourself, *"What would be the most exciting, fun and joyous thing to do right this minute?"*

That is the thing to do next.

You see, it is our nature as human beings to joyfully create. It is our nature to take action, to dream dreams and to manifest those dreams. And the thing that keeps us from doing this is the conditioning we have received that says it's not possible. Or worse, that if we reach for our dreams we'll be punished (I probably don't need to say it, but if you feel that—change that belief right away!).

Once we are back in alignment with our true nature, and we focus purely and simply on our dream, we know instantly what would be the most fun to *do* towards that dream. So slow down, keep dreaming, and above all else have fun on the way to the receiving. That, after all, is really what it's all about.

REMEMBER, ACT BUT DON'T "EARN"

All of conscious creation and especially the "action" step should be elegant and easy. It should feel more like *receiving* than earning. Have you ever heard someone complain that "given how hard they have worked" they *should* have thus and such by now? *That's entitlement, which comes from feeling that you have to "earn" the good things coming to you.*

Keep this in mind as you go about your actions. The minute they feel more like "to-do" lists than genuinely inspired and exciting actions, you have crossed over into earning.

How can you tell when you're trying to *earn* your reality rather than receive it? Well, the fun will be gone for one thing. You can always tell when you are on the right track by how you *feel*. If you're filled with joy and having a blast, keep it up. But when the joy fades and your action plan feels like a chore, you are probably *earning*.

Here's another clue: if you catch yourself thinking things like, *"If I do this many techniques and take this many actions, I will get my dream."*

Although techniques and actions are a *part of the process* of conscious creating, they are not the *cause* of the creations. The *resonance* that emits from *you* is the cause of creation. The techniques and actions are merely a way to help you to shift that resonance.

What do you do when you cross that line? Forgive yourself. Check for a possible belief, and move back into actions of inspired joy.

ACTIONS UNRELATED TO YOUR DREAM

The actions you take do not always have to relate directly to your dream. In fact, some of the most powerful actions are more related to loving and honoring yourself.

One of the biggest obstacles to conscious creation for nearly everyone is a feeling of *"I don't deserve."* This is why The Map begins with reminding you of your divinity. You *do* deserve... by the very nature of your being.

But most of us have been stifled, shamed, ridiculed and otherwise reminded of our (perceived) shortcomings our entire lives. *"I deserve an easy, elegant life of my dreams"* is not a phrase we grew up with. Changing these self-images and beliefs is part of what you will do over time.

And action towards this end works wonders.

What might those actions look like? Honoring yourself and taking baby steps towards the life you want to live. Such as:

> *Give yourself one afternoon a week to do **only** what*
> *you enjoy. If it's staring out the window...stare out*

the window. If it's playing video games...play video games. Don't judge it. Just enjoy it. Know you are headed towards a life in which you will do only *what you enjoy one hundred percent of the time. (And if a nasty 'ol belief pops into your head and you think, "If I allow myself to do what I want one hundred percent of the time I will never do anything."— change it!)*

Stay in bed for one entire day. OK, so maybe you'll get bored and get up. But give yourself the permission to stay in bed. The average person on this planet lives 24,528 days. Few of us give ourselves permission to do absolutely nothing for even one *of those days unless we are ill. Be the exception. Expand the idea that you are absolutely* free *to do whatever you desire.*

Make a list of twenty-five things you love to do. (I have done this. It amazed me that the vast majority of things I love cost very little or nothing at all.) Do one of those things. Make a commitment to yourself to do one regularly. Know you are honoring who you are and who you are becoming by making time and space for the things you love.

Say "no" when you really don't feel like doing what someone wants you to do. Say it with kindness. And say it knowing it is self-loving to honor your own desires and needs.

Organize your closet, clean out your drawers, decorate a room or buy yourself a new item of clothing. Do something that makes your life more enjoyable. As you do this, reaffirm your intent to create a beautiful, loving, supportive life for yourself.

When I was beginning this journey, I didn't have money to spend on new clothes or re-decorating my home. But when I reflected upon what really made me happy, a lovely environment was at the top of the list.

And so were flowers. One action I began to take for myself was splurging on fresh flowers every week. The ten-dollar expenditure was a stretch for my budget. But I did it anyway...as a statement to the universe that I deserved beauty and elegance.

It wasn't long afterward that money began to flow. And before long, money was no longer an issue in my life. After moving into the home of my (then) dreams, a neighbor stopped by and offered to plant flowers in my yard. She created a heaven on earth in my front and backyard...overflowing pots, water fountains and even a "moon garden" with white, night-blooming flowers that reflected the light of the moon. Now, several "home of my dreams" later, the same friend creates amazing fresh flower arrangements that fill my home with beauty and fragrance every week.

I never look at those amazing blooms without feeling grateful for their beauty, my friend's stunning artistic talent, and the universe, for responding to my *self-love* with *more things to love*...all those years ago.

Take action towards the life you love...in little ways at first. But trust me; the little ways will morph before your very eyes into bigger and bigger ways...should you allow it.

THE SCARY ACTIONS

Sometimes the action you most need to take will scare the hell out of you. You will come to the realization that something or someone in your life is an excuse to not grow up, take responsibility for your life or be all you can be. And you will *know*...the most loving thing you can do, for you *and* for them, is to move on.

Most often these actions involve moving on from a job, a relationship and/or a living arrangement. If you are contemplating one of these, there are a few things to remember:

1. **Don't rush into anything.** Major life changes deserve the time and space to both think and feel them out. If something is not going well in your life, taking action to get "away" from that thing won't change much. If you don't change yourself first, chances are you'll create the same situation again. It will be in a different time and space and maybe with different players, but it will *feel* exactly the same.

And often, when you change *yourself*, the *players* in your life miraculously change. I've seen this happen over and over again with bosses, partners, spouses and children. On the other hand...

2. **Don't postpone the inevitable.** If you are in an abusive situation, get out. If you *know* you don't belong in a certain place, don't waste years of your life before you make the move. Do what you need to do. It will help to remember...

3. **Self-loving actions are also loving to others.** Many people don't take actions they know they should take because of how they think it will affect others, be it their children, their employees, their co-workers, their partners or their parents. But know this, the actions you take for yourself, motivated out of self-love, will *always* affect others more positively than negatively.

Of course this applies differently to children than it does to adults. We do "owe" the children we bring into this world a certain level of protection, love and guidance while they are young. But to remain with a spouse "for the sake of the children" shows them an example of how to be a martyr instead of how to create a life they adore. Remember they learn from you.

And to postpone your happiness for the "sake" of another adult is codependent. What message are you sending them? The message is: *"You are not strong enough, smart enough or whatever enough to function on your own."* Ouch. That doesn't sound very loving.

If you are concerned about how an action you wish to take will affect others, the most loving thing you can do is to hold the intention and the vision that the change you make will affect them in only positive ways.

Can I do that?

Yes. You can. And you can make the change with kindness, compassion and love. But before you take these actions...

4. **Align your beliefs.** Your beliefs got you into the reality you now want to change. Take a very close look at how you created what you did and make the changes you know you need to make. Then and only then...

5. **Dream the result.** Decide how people will react. Decide how smoothly it will go. Choose not just the action but the response of your world to this action. And be ready, because...

6. **The universe *will* respond.** Sometimes the universe will respond slowly, sometimes rapidly. But it *will* respond and you may be surprised at the speed of the response.

One young man I know had worked in his family's online business for ten years. It was safe, secure and comfortable. But it wasn't his bliss.

However the thought of venturing out and finding something of his own was petrifying. And he needed the money the job brought in to survive. Over the years he half-heartedly tried to find other work, but never made the leap.

Until one day, he could take it no more. He lovingly told his family he had to move on. It was a bittersweet victory, as he liked being around his family and they liked being around him.

The very next day, he was inspired out of the blue to make a call to a company that did the work he loved and within a week, had landed the job of his dreams.

Would that have happened anyway? I doubt it. Sometimes you need to make space for what you want to drop in.

But you are still responsible for taking the next step...

7. **Dream the *new* life you desire.** When we close the door on an old creation, we often need time to mourn. It is, after all, the death of what was once your dream. But after you've said your goodbyes and closed those

doors, the real work still lies ahead. You must create what it is you *do* truly desire.

Now don't just sit there—take an action step towards that dream of yours today!

LIFE-ALTERING TAKEAWAYS

Read these slowly. Meditate on them or sit and contemplate them. Let them in. Let them change you.

+ Action is a proving ground. When you have clarified the desire and given the desire energy, taking action should feel positive. If it doesn't, you need to go back and understand *why*. If taking action doesn't feel good, or you aren't motivated to take action, something is wrong and needs tending to.

+ Action intensifies the energies and speeds up the manifestation. If you felt joyous about what you wanted and believed you could have it, you would want to get out there and begin doing it, preparing for it, taking steps towards it, etc. Those actions create more positive energy, which allows your reality to shift, creating what you want sooner!

+ Action should be part of the *fun*. The old adage, *"It's not about the destination it's about the journey,"* is a critically important concept in manifesting your dreams. It's the energy of the fun, excitement and fulfillment you feel along the way that draws to you the reality you desire. You know you are on the right path when the journey towards your dreams is a blast!

+ Although techniques and actions are a *part of the process* of conscious creating, they are not the *cause* of the creations. The cause is the *resonance* you emit. The techniques and actions are merely a way to help you to shift that resonance.

+ The universe will never deny you. *You* may deny you, though.

YOUR NEXT STEPS

☐ Make a list of twenty-five things you love to do. Do one of them.

☐ Sit quietly and get in touch with the essence of one of your desires. Feel the joy and excitement. Imagine you could not fail. What would be the most exciting and joyful next steps?

☐ Prepare a plan of action for at least one of your dreams.

☐ Intend to implement that plan by a certain date and write down that promise in your journal.

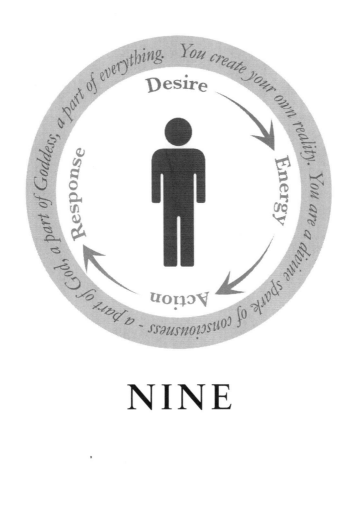

NINE

YOUR REALITY WILL RESPOND

*"Listen to your life.
It's showing you everything you
need to know about who you can become."*

—RICHARD BACH

Now comes the *really* fun part...watching your world respond!

It is important to understand that your world is *always* responding to you. Your personal reality is an exact reflection of the energy you put out. So it should make sense that when you change your energy flow you should see your world change, right?

This is why it is imperative to pay attention to the changes in your reality. If you don't pay attention, how will you know if you are "flowing" energy that's in alignment with your desires?

Remember, in this three-dimensional world it takes time for things to manifest. Generally what you desire will not *fully* manifest right away, especially if you have big dreams. And if you don't pay attention and you don't see the signs, it is too easy to think, "It isn't working."

But it always works. And if you stay conscious, you can *see* it working, which will strengthen your belief in the concept that you can consciously create.

The best news is you don't even have to wait for long! With any powerful technique you should see *a sign* that it's working within several days. By powerful technique I mean one that you put a lot of emotion behind. Several days is nothing, right? How long have you stayed in your current reality... months, years, decades?

So, when you're actively working on creating your reality, pay attention to *everything* in your world. And look for signs everywhere.

WHAT IS A "SIGN"?

A sign is a *change in your reality that relates to the area of life you are trying to improve.* If you do a technique to create more money, the sign will relate to money. If you are trying to attract a partner, your sign will relate to relationships, etc.

WHAT DOES A SIGN LOOK LIKE?

A sign can be tiny or big. Generally they are tiny in the beginning. A sign can be subtle, or in your face. Usually they are quite subtle. The biggest challenge is to recognize them for what they are—indications that your new resonance is changing your physical reality.

Here are some examples of signs:

If you intend to create more money, a sign might look like one of these:

- You find a penny on the sidewalk.
- You reach into a pair of pants you haven't worn for a while and find some cash.
- You turn on the TV and catch news coverage of a local

lottery winner.

- You get a bigger tax refund than you expected.
- A friend invites you to dinner and picks up the check.
- You run into an old friend and they tell you of the huge promotion they just received.
- Your neighbor drops by with an armful of zucchini from her garden.
- You find an old ring you thought you'd lost.
- You win a bottle of wine from a raffle at the benefit dinner you attend.
- You receive an email with a twenty percent off coupon for the birthday gift you'd planned on buying your mother.

If you intend to create a loving relationship, a sign might look like one of these:

- Your best friend calls and excitedly tells you about his engagement.
- You are waiting in line at the supermarket and *Brides* magazine falls off the display rack in front of you.
- A co-worker you are not particularly attracted to asks you for a date.
- A person at the gym asks you for your number, but never calls.
- You read a headline on your Internet home page titled, "Married couples today happier than ten years ago."
- You have brunch at your favorite restaurant and see a wedding party taking photographs on the lawn.

- The pharmacist flirts with you when you fill a prescription.
- Your mother calls and tells you she dreamt you got married.
- You see a car go by with a "Just Married" sign on the back.
- You turn on the radio and "At Last" is playing.

Are you beginning to get the picture? A sign is related to the area of life you are trying to manifest and it is ultimately good news.

HOW DO YOU RESPOND TO THE SIGNS?

How you respond to signs in your world is critical. This is the place where people screw up their realties more than at any other time in the manifestation process. Most people respond to signs with no energy because they don't see them for what they are. And even worse, many respond with negative energy or "flow-stoppers" because they think they aren't *attracting* their dream.

If you learn anything at all from this book, learn how to respond to signs in a way that supports your dream.

Here are some common mistakes people make when responding to signs from the universe like those described above. I've also included alternate responses that will not kill the flow but *support* it instead:

The intention: I intend unlimited cash and resources to flow into my life easily, and abundantly.

The signs from your reality that you are creating it:

- **You find a penny on the sidewalk.**

   Common response: *Look at that. A penny. That will buy me a lot of nothing. Not even worth bending over to pick it up.*

   Flow strengthening response: *Hey, a penny! (You pick it up.) I* know *this is a sign that my intention to have greater abundance is working…if I can create a penny I can create a billion pennies!*

- **You reach into a pair of pants you haven't worn for a while and find some cash.**

   Common response: *Hey, I forgot this money was here. Could it be a sign? Nah…after all it was my money to begin with—it's not like it's new money. I am such a space cadet, I can't even keep track of the money I have, let alone create more.*

   Flow strengthening response: *Yahoo! Cash I didn't even know I had! I wonder if this really was mine, or if it manifested here out of thin air just because I'm working on abundance? Either way, I'm sure it's a* *sign my flow is headed in the right direction!*

- **You turn on the TV and catch news coverage of a local lottery winner.**

  Common response: *Geez. Lucky son of a gun. Why couldn't that be me?*

  Flow strengthening response: *Wow...look at that! This must be a sign for me! I am drawing others to me who have received abundance because my flow is changing! I'm going to strengthen my flow and do another focusing technique right now!*

- **You get a bigger tax refund than you expected.**

  Common response: *Yeah, I'm getting $100 more than I'd thought...but the $750 total won't go very far given the bills I have stacked up right now.*

  Flow strengthening response: *One hundred dollars of abundance just arrived in my life! Yesterday it wasn't here, today it is. I made this happen, I know I did! More money must be on its way to me...this has to be a sign! It's going to be fantastic to have money flowing to me like I'm turning on a faucet!*

- **A friend invites you to dinner and picks up the check.**

Common response: *Oh, man, he picked up the check again! I hate seeing myself through his eyes...poor and needy. When am I ever going to be able to pay him back for all these dinners?*

Flow strengthening response: *Wow. I just created a wonderful and free dinner. I know this friend always pays, that's not new. What is new is that I am finally owning my piece of this..."I" created this generous friend and this abundance!*

· **You run into an old friend and they tell you of the huge promotion they just received.**

Common response: *Dammit. Why do good things happen to everyone but me? I wish I had a promotion like that. Why not me, universe?*

Flow strengthening response: *Anytime I see someone around me who has wonderful things happen it is a whisper to me that my life can be that good or better. That I ran into this person with great news is a sign my own abundance is about to increase!!*

· **Your neighbor drops by with an armful of zucchini from her garden.**

Common response: *Zucchini—the crabgrass of vegetables. What on earth am I going to do with* *twenty-five pounds of zucchini?*

Flow strengthening response: *Wow. This is a sign of abundance, isn't it? Zucchini is energy just like money. If I can create an abundance of zucchini, I can create an abundance of money!*

- **You find an old ring you thought you'd lost.**

  Common response: *Huh. I thought I lost this. Darn. If I'd known I'd find it I wouldn't have gone out and replaced it. I could really use the money I spent on that new ring right now.*

  Flow strengthening response: *Look at that! I'm richer today and this is proof! This must be a sign. I'm going to go do another technique!*

- **You win a bottle of wine from a raffle at the benefit dinner you attend.**

  Common response: *How useless is this? I don't even drink wine.*

  Flow strengthening response: *Look at that...I can't keep abundance from coming to me! Another sign! I think I'll save this to bring to a dinner party sometime and I won't have to go out and buy one...it is like money in the bank!*

- You receive an email with a twenty percent off coupon for the birthday gift you'd planned on buying your mother.

  Common response: *This will come in handy for Mom's present. I suppose I could take this as a sign but that's stupid. It's not like I got cash. And I get these emails every week from this store—I would have gotten this even if I weren't focusing on abundance.*

  Flow strengthening response: *Yahoo! Saved ten dollars today! Yet another sign...the way this is going I should be seeing much bigger signs in the not too distant future. Seeing these signs really helps me to be patient because I see the energy shifting, so I just need to hold this energy and know I am abundant!*

Lets look at the relationship signs:

The intention: I intend to create a loving relationship with someone in which we both feel greater and greater levels of peace, safety, fun, freedom, ease, joy, intimacy, vulnerability, trust, play, creativity, expansion, tenderness and love.

The signs from your reality that you are creating it:

- **Your best friend calls and excitedly tells you about his engagement.**

Common response: *Damn he is lucky. I bet he'll bring her to our class reunion and now I won't have anyone to hang out with.*

Flow strengthening response: *This is fantastic! For someone so close to me to create such wonderful news about a relationship must mean I'm really close to manifesting "the one" for me!! I think I may be more excited about this than he is!!*

· **You are waiting in line at the supermarket and *Brides* magazine falls off the display rack in front of you.**

Common response: *Stupid people! Always putting magazines back in the wrong places.*

Flow strengthening response: *Oh my. Look at that. What are the odds? I think my reality is trying to tell me something. I'm getting closer to the relationship I am dreaming of!*

· **A co-worker you are not particularly attracted to asks you for a date.**

Common response: *I ask for the man of my dreams and I get the man from Nerdsville. Great. Just my luck.*

Flow strengthening response: *Well, hey, he isn't the man of my dreams but he's a man who is interested in me. That is a step in the right direction. Now to make sure my order is crystal clear, I'm going to take another look at my intentions and clarify how I want to feel with my "dream man" in every regard.*

· **A person at the gym asks you for your number, but never calls.**

Common response: *I wonder why he didn't call? Maybe he thinks I'm too fat? Or maybe I acted like a dork when he asked for my number?*

Flow strengthening response: *I am so excited! I am putting out flow for the perfect guy for me and it's working! Yeah, gym-guy didn't call but who cares? He was probably just a sign that I'm getting closer to my dream. The universe is totally cued into the essence I want and I trust that!*

· **You read a headline on your internet home page titled, "Married couples today happier than ten years ago."**

Common response: *No wonder there aren't any good girls/guys left to date anymore...they're all happily married!*

Flow strengthening response: *That headline is a great sign that my intention is becoming manifest! I know my flow brought that article to me!*

- You have brunch at your favorite restaurant and see a wedding party taking photographs on the lawn.

  Common response: *Geez. Way to ruin my perfect Saturday brunch. Now instead of enjoying my meal I'm thinking, "Why not me?"*

  Flow strengthening response: *Gosh, what are the chances I would pick this day and time to have brunch here? Thank you universe! I know this "coincidence" is not a coincidence at all, but a "sign" that my dream is becoming manifest!*

- The pharmacist flirts with you when you fill a prescription.

  Common response: *These guys are all talk and no action. He's probably married. Men!*

  Flow strengthening response: *I must be putting out the vibe. One more sign means one more step towards a lifetime of joy with the man of my dreams. Nice!*

- Your mother calls and tells you she dreamt you got married.

Common response: *She's probably judging me for still being single. Doesn't she know I've been trying all these years? Something must be wrong with me.*

Flow strengthening response: *This is totally trippy. Even my mom is giving me signs now!*

· **You see a car go by with a "Just Married" sign on the back.**

Common response: *Sucker. Probably end in divorce. Happily ever after is a fairy tale.*

Flow strengthening response: *This can only mean one thing: I'm next!*

· **You turn on the radio and "At Last" is playing.**

Common response: *This makes me so sad. Everyone finds their true love but me...*

Flow strengthening response: *I can't–sorry–I mean I can totally believe this! My energy shifts and everywhere I look I see a sign that I'm about to receive my heart's desire. I'm going to imagine her/ him in bed snuggled next to me tonight. Oh this feels so good!*

Do you now see why the way you respond to signs is so important? All that emotion is either strengthening or weakening your creation.

WHAT SHOULD YOU DO WHEN YOU RECEIVE A SIGN?

First, celebrate!

When you receive a sign get excited—do a mental happy dance!! This is *great* news! A sign indicates that your flow of positive energy towards your desire is working! When you acknowledge your success, even a little bit, you strengthen the belief that you can consciously create your reality, which increases the flow, which further increases the signs! It's a positive spiral!

Shouldn't I wait until *my dream* has totally manifested to celebrate?

Why? This is the most exciting part! Your first signs! Your first indications that you are on the right track to consciously create what you want. By the time it manifests, it won't be *as* exciting because you will be *used* to feeling as though you already have it. Celebrate now, *and* later!

Then own what you made happen

You shifted your world. Let that in. Give yourself time to allow this truth to sink in. You. Have. Changed. Your. Physical. Reality.

Allow that to rock your world a bit.

Then (maybe), refine your dream

Your sign may have told you something about your dream. You may want to take that information and incorporate some changes into it.

For instance, in the above example, you desire a loving relationship and your co-worker asks you for a date—and the idea of dating him/her appalls you.

This positive sign may have caused you to think about how you can further refine your dream. And you can then add, "I intend to create a relationship with mutual physical attraction," to your list of intentions.

It is not necessary to tweak your dream when you receive a sign, but if the sign happens to clarify your desire, by all means change your intention.

And also (maybe) step it up a notch!

When positive signs show up, you may want to use the momentum and excitement to strengthen your flow even further. You may want to do your techniques more often or take more action towards your dream. You've done a great job flowing energy and this is the time to make sure you keep it up!

And absolutely *expect* your dream to fully manifest

It's one thing to get excited about signs showing up, it's another to take it to the next level and truly *expect* your dream to manifest. Please recognize that if you can create one thing consciously, you can create *anything* consciously. You *can* do this. And your dream will come, if you keep holding the flow.

Expect it to come. Get ready for it. But don't forget...conscious creation is an everyday practice. One success doesn't guarantee the next. Each and every day you need to consciously step into the resonance of that self you want to be, the one who *has* the dream.

WHAT SHOULDN'T YOU DO WHEN YOU RECEIVE A "SIGN"?

Don't blow it off

It is tempting to see signs and be disappointed because your full desire hasn't manifested yet, especially when you are new at conscious creation. You're going to have to be extremely disciplined with yourself to make sure this doesn't happen. A sign is phenomenal news. But you'll have to train yourself... first to *see* it, and then to see it as something *great*.

Don't give it to your ego (aka negative self)

Yes, you did consciously create (a sign, anyway). But it doesn't make you better than those who haven't. It doesn't make you special. Different, maybe. But not better than.

Don't share the news with those who will not honor it

Even if you are a seasoned reality creator, this is a *new* dream. Or at least a newly born dream. It's still fragile. Treat it with the care you would treat any newborn. Keep it away from those who would kill it.

Don't let it freak you out

Especially in the beginning, watching dreams manifest before your eyes will challenge much of your former view of reality. Suddenly, the "cause and effect" world you used to believe in becomes so much more.

On top of that, all the stories you've told yourself about who you are suddenly aren't true and you are faced with the truth.

You are *powerful*.

It can seem like too much responsibility. You can feel undeserving. It can be overwhelming.

If you are faced with these feelings, understand that they are perfectly normal. And know you are not alone. Your unseen friends are with you, supporting you and guiding you. And the more you *ask* for their help, the more they will be *able* to help.

You may feel that your world is changing much too fast—that your new realities are manifesting too quickly. It is OK to take a break from this work. You may need space to integrate the changes, or a pause to allow new dreams to flow in. Simply ask your higher self to slow things down a bit. And ask for their help in integrating this new "you" and the new world you find yourself in.

AND WHAT IF THE "SIGN" IS NEGATIVE?

Yes, it can happen. Sometimes your intention is to receive something and you manifest just the opposite. For example, if you flow energy towards having more money and your reality responds with *no* positive signs and unexpected bills, obviously something is amiss.

I can hear your thoughts, *"Seriously?! Why even do this if it can make my reality worse than when I started?"*

Calm down. This can happen if you are flowing more negative than positive energy. And you can change that *and thus, your world.*

WHY WOULD YOU SEE
ONLY NEGATIVE SIGNS?

You may have pretty much ignored your thoughts and feelings until now. Suddenly you may be thinking a great deal more about particular areas of your life, hoping for them to change. If negative *feelings* come up when you think about these things, you may be putting out more energy for the thing you *don't* want than the thing you do.

If you want to create more money, but when you write your intentions and flow energy you worry about not having enough money, you will create what you *don't* want. If you desire a loving relationship but every time you think about it you feel sad because you don't have one, you are creating what you *don't* want.

If this is happening to you, you probably have one or more beliefs that won't allow you to manifest what you desire. I suggest reviewing chapter five and ferreting out any hidden beliefs that won't allow a reality as good as your dream.

Sometimes we have limits as to what we believe we can create, or how good reality can get. Sometimes we have deep-seated beliefs that we will be punished if we want too much, or get "too big for our britches."

It may scare you when signs are negative. But you have everything you need in this book to understand why this is happening and to change the beliefs that are causing your reality. If you don't believe that, make that your first belief to change.

And you can always tell if you are flowing positive energy by simply asking yourself how you feel. Feeling good flows positive energy; feeling bad flows negative energy. It's that simple.

AND SOMETIMES WHAT LOOKS LIKE A NEGATIVE SIGN MAY BE A BLESSING IN DISGUISE

What often appears to be bad news can simply be the fastest way for the universe to manifest your dream. You've heard the stories: the loss of a job that opens the door to a far better job, or a breakup that opens the door to a more profoundly loving relationship.

When I was growing my marketing company, there were many "blessings in disguise." My mantra was *"No matter what happens, it's going to turn out great."*

Here's one example: In my first year of business, my only product was postcards. When Thanksgiving rolled around, one of my best clients wanted to send greeting cards. I found affordable Thanksgiving greeting cards for her and offered them to several other clients as well.

Two weeks before Thanksgiving, the cards still hadn't arrived. I put in a panicked call to my supplier. He asked, *"Didn't you receive our email? That card has been discontinued."* This was devastating news! But only for a moment.

Ultimately the bad news forced me to hire a designer and print my own. My greeting card line was born, and I ultimately sold hundreds of thousands of cards.

But this brings up the question: *Would my reality have turned out as well if I had responded differently to that bad news?*

I don't think it would have. Your response to your world is critical, folks. Stay conscious and respond in ways that support your dream.

My life now has almost no "bad" news. Years of changing beliefs and strengthening my expectation of only good news has made a huge difference. But if and when it does, I will still respond with *"No matter what happens, it's going to turn out great."*

AND IF YOU'RE GETTING BOTH POSITIVE AND NEGATIVE SIGNS?

Honestly, receiving positive and negative signs is what will happen most often. And this usually means that is you haven't held the resonance long enough. Creation on this planet takes time. To make changes in your world, you have to hold the feeling of having it long enough for it to manifest.

What is *long enough*? It varies with the creation. But rest assured, you don't have to hold a positive resonance *perfectly*. Positive thoughts and feelings are vastly more powerful than negative thoughts and feelings. And any step in a positive direction will benefit your reality.

If you receive both positive and negative signs make sure you pay the *most* attention to the positive signs and respond with "flow strengthening" thoughts. But if the negative signs don't dissipate, or if the positive signs aren't increasing in number, take another look at your beliefs.

Everyone has beliefs that need to change if they want to live a life they absolutely love. As you know, beliefs are the cornerstone to creation. Always be on the lookout for what your reality is telling you about yours.

THE PARADOX OF PATIENCE

It is *imperative* to have patience while waiting for your dreams to manifest. And by patience I don't mean *passive* patience such as sitting around waiting for your boat to come in, your prince to arrive or even your intentions to manifest.

I mean *engaged* patience. Engaged patience is holding the *feeling of already having what you want* without focusing on the fact that you *don't have it yet*—and doing that *patiently* until it manifests.

Easier said than done.

Most people start thinking about the fact they *don't* have their dream, and their resonance does a nose dive. All the great energy they created by flowing positive thoughts and emotions goes right out the window.

Paradoxically, with practice you may not need patience at all. Because if you really *can* feel as if you already have the thing you want, you are no longer concerned about it manifesting. Because in your mind, *you already have it.*

And when you are in *that* state, your dreams will become reality in the quickest, easiest and most elegant way possible.

WHEN YOUR DREAM FULLY MANIFESTS

When that great day comes, in which a dream you've been working on is finally here, by all means, celebrate your triumph! But after the champagne has been drunk and the confetti has been swept away, take some time to reflect and *respond.*

It is probably even *more* important to respond appropriately *after* the dream manifests than *before*, when you are only seeing signs. Why?

If you don't, you run the risk of un-creating it.

What? No! Please say that can't happen!

It happens all the time. Look at your world. How many lottery winners have won millions only to wind up broke just a few years later? How many famous stars (movie, sports, music) have self-destructed after a meteoric rise to fame?

I've seen it happen often on a smaller scale also. One man was euphoric that his entire life had changed as a result of taking my seminars. He became engaged and landed a much better job, and his investments were paying double what they usually paid.

And just a few short months later his investments had taken a nosedive, his engagement fell apart and he lost his job. Why does this happen?

Because these people did not *continue* to see themselves as successful, wealthy or loved, their image of themselves snapped back to how they thought of themselves prior to their "win." And reality always follows the energetic vibration we emit. Always.

But if you are proactive, you don't have to be one of those people. Here are some suggestions to ensure that your "newly born realities" will thrive:

TAKE RESPONSIBILITY FOR IT

You created it. Own it. Don't let your negative self tell you it would have happened anyway, that it was just fate, or luck.

Also, don't let your negative self tell you are somehow *better than* others for creating it.

Your negative self may try to tell you that it wasn't really you—that your unseen friends created it or that someone in the physical world created it for you. Maybe you *did* receive help, either from physical friends or unseen friends. That's not the point.

The point is *you* created it in *your* world. Spend some time letting that in. Allow it to strengthen your belief that you *create your own reality*.

SHIFT YOUR SELF-IMAGE

You are not the same person you were before you created this success. You have changed. You could not have created it without changing. Somehow you held the resonance that you could and would have this piece of your dream. And you were right. It manifested in your world.

The way to keep it in your world is to continue to expand your self-image. Don't shrink back into your old self. How could that happen? It could happen if fear creeps in and you start to worry about losing your dream. It could happen if you began to think of yourself as powerless again, as someone who has no ability to change your world.

Be proactive. Here are some suggestions:

Work with your child and adolescent selves

These aspects of you may be afraid that they don't have what it takes to keep this success in their lives and they are right. They don't. So go and spend some time with them and let them know *they* don't have to live this success. They need to stay in their world and you, the strong, powerful, spiritual adult will handle *your* world. Give them whatever they want in their world, but make them promise to stay there.

Work with your negative self.

Remember your negative self seeks to sabotage you. And when you are shaky with a new reality, it will have the perfect opening to try and tear you down. Head it off at the pass by spending some time with it every day.

It doesn't have to be long, three to five minutes will do. Imagine it standing or sitting next to you and dialogue with it. Tell it about your recent success.

It may sound something like this:

> Me: *"I am almost finished with the book. My editor is excited about it and thinks it's going to be quite a success."*

NS: *"And you believe her?"*

Me: *"Yes, I do. I have no reason to think she would lie."*

NS: *"You're quite naive aren't you?"*

Me: *"No not really. I am holding an intention for it to be a success."*

NS: *"I've got news for you, baby. You are not only naive, you are stupid. How many books like this are out there already?"*

Me: *"None written by me."*

NS: *"And you honestly think that will make a difference? Give it up. You lucked out once with your marketing company and now you think you can create another multimillion dollar business? You are loony toons. You are a talentless Pollyanna. No one will listen to you or learn from you. Forget about the book and go volunteer at a homeless shelter. Those are people you can relate to."*

Me: *"Are you finished?"*

NS: *"No. What kind of wife leaves her husband*

for days on end to finish her book? A terrible wife, that's who. You have the luck of the Irish, girl, if he doesn't leave you for this."

Me: *"Are you finished now?"*

NS: *"No. I'm not finished. You are getting old and fat sitting around writing all day. This book is ruining your life."*

Me: *"Are you finished now?"*

NS: *"No. You are also a horrible mother and friend—you're so selfish. You will be very lucky if you don't die a long horrible death alone.*

Me: *"Are you finished now?"*

NS: *"Yes."*

Me: *"Thank you for sharing. Higher self, please come and wrap my negative self in love and light and take it away for healing."*

Let it be as brutal as you can. Don't censor it. When it is finished, you will feel much lighter, and you won't be carrying around the toxic energy that will poison your flow.

Remember, this exercise can be done during the man-ifestation process as well. It really is amazing how well it works.

Be on the lookout for "sabotaging beliefs"

These beliefs might be:

This is too good to be true.

When things get really good, the other shoe will fall.

If I get too big for my britches, something will happen to take me down.

I don't deserve a reality this good.

Pride goeth before a fall.

And, of course, change them!!

Be vigilant about protecting your newly owned power

Share your successes only with people who will support you and your dream. Surround yourself with positive people, read books that solidify your knowing of conscious creation, and ask for help regularly from your unseen friends.

It's just a matter of energy and time. If you can hold the positive flow long enough, your desire *will* manifest. It has to. That's the way the universe works.

Dream the next dream

Once you have manifested your dream or even a good chunk of your dream, it is important to dream a new dream. Ask yourself, *"How does it get better than this?"*

> *If you created your dream job, your new dream may be more creativity at work, more connectedness with co-workers, more successes at your job or more fun and joy.*

> *If you created your dream relationship, your new dream may be greater depths of intimacy, love, caring and joy.*

> *If you created your dream home, your new dream may be to fill that home with the sparkling energies of love, joy and growth. Or you may dream of filling it with beautiful furnishings, decorative touches and plants.*

If you don't have something new to create you may re-create something old. I've witnessed people (myself included) create a dream falling apart, just so they could create the same thing all over again.

You came to earth to experience your "divine creative capacity." You *want* to create. You *need* a dream.

So when your dream manifests, definitely enjoy it! And dream a new dream too.

And take my word for it, life can always get better.

LIFE-ALTERING TAKE AWAYS

Read these slowly. Meditate on them or sit and contemplate them. Let them in. Let them change you.

+ Your world is *always* responding to you. Your personal reality is an absolute mirror that reflects exactly the energy you put out. This is why it is imperative to pay attention to how your reality responds to your shifts and changes as you begin to consciously create. If you don't pay attention, how will you know you are "flowing" energy that is in alignment with your desires?

+ With any powerful technique you should see a sign within several days, that will let you know it's working. When you are actively working on conscious creation, pay attention to *everything* in your world.

+ Once you see the sign(s)...*expect* that the full manifestation is going to happen! It's one thing to get excited about signs showing up, it's another to take it to the next level and truly *expect* your dream to manifest.

+ Share your successes *only* with people who will support you and your dream. Surround yourself with positive people, read books that solidify your knowing of conscious creation, and ask for help regularly from your unseen friends.

✦ It may scare you when signs are negative. But you have *everything* you need in this book to figure out *why* this is happening and to change the beliefs that are causing your reality. If you don't believe that, make *that* your first belief to change.

✦ Paradoxically, with practice you may not need patience at all. Because if you really *can* feel as if you already have the thing you want, you are no longer concerned about it manifesting. Because in your mind, *you already have it.* And when you are in *that* state, your dreams will become reality in the quickest, easiest and most elegant way possible.

YOUR NEXT STEPS

☐ If you have done a technique in the past few days, write down the signs that have manifested in your world as a result.

☐ Check out the conscious creation success stories of others (and also post your own) at http://www.livealifey-oulove.com/inspire/

☐ If you have not done a technique in the past few days, review chapter seven and do one of the following:

> **A Day in the Day of the Dream**
> **Make the Movie Real**
> **Grateful for "Now and Then"**

Over the next three days, make a note in your journal of any signs that show up.

TEN

THE SECRET TO FASTER CHANGE

"We are what we think.
All that we are arises with our thoughts.
With our thoughts we make the world."

—BUDDHA

OK, you've discovered that you are the creator of your entire universe! You have written your intentions and you flow positive energy towards those intentions every day. You take action towards your dreams and watch carefully for signs that prove your dreams are becoming manifest.

What now?

Well, if you worked on your dream for half an hour each day and did nothing during the other 23 hours but wait for your dream, everything would be cool. Your dream would manifest because nothing is opposing it. It's just a matter of time.

But no one does that. We have *thoughts* all day every day and we have *emotions* with those thoughts. And some of them aren't pretty. And if they're not pretty, they are stealing your dream.

What? Do you mean I could work on my dream diligently and still not get it?

I didn't say that. If you follow The Map you *will* get your dream. But The Map is not just a method to manifest your dreams. The Map is a *way of life*.

It's a way of existing in your world, knowing you are manifesting your reality anew, each and every day. It is a way of *being* in your world, and being responsible *for* your world.

And the secret to allowing the changes in your reality in the quickest and most elegant way possible, is this sixth step of The Map: *Stay in joy—as if you had the dream.*

Let's look at the first part of this step: *Stay in joy.* How do you do that?

Well, you could monitor your thoughts every minute of every day. But with thousands of thoughts a day, this could become a bit challenging. And the truth is, there is no need to monitor your thoughts. You can keep your resonance positive with one simple tool...

MONITOR THE WAY YOU *FEEL*

Your goal is to be happy one hundred percent of the time.

Aw, come on, is anyone *happy* all *the time?*

Yes. And you can be too. It will take time. But if being happy all of the time is your intention, you can create it. You begin by realizing that happiness is a *choice.*

"CHOOSE" TO BE HAPPY

Don't wait until you have your dream. Honestly, your dream won't give it to you anyway. Be happy *now.*

Why spend one more day not being happy? It's just not worth wasting your life on feeling sad, disappointed, discouraged or any other negative emotion.

Also (this is big, pay attention), *anything but happy will drain the flow off your dream.*

Not happy brings more things to be not happy about. Do you get that? Happy attracts more happy.

The Law of Attraction is true. And once your beliefs are in alignment with your dream, the only thing that will stop your dream is spending days on end in a pity party or other such nonsense.

Your emotions count, folks. Big time. May as well make it easier on yourself from here on out and just choose to *be happy.*

Come on, it can't be that easy. If it were why don't more people choose happiness?

Because most people have it ass-backwards. They think the *things* are going to bring them *happiness*...the job, the love, the money, the house, whatever. But it's our *emotions* that create these realities. Be happy first. Then dream the dream. Then be even happier!

For some, happiness *is* just a simple choice. Others may have a belief embedded such as:

Circumstances create my happiness.

Simply change it to:

I create my happiness.

But even *after* you've changed the belief, you still need to make the *choice* each and every day.

But what if bad things are happening...like an accident, or an illness, or being served with divorce papers?

If you are faced with difficult or even devastating challenges, happiness may *not* be a choice for a while. If you are dealing with sudden bad news, it is appropriate and healthy to feel your emotions without censorship or suppression. Your creation work can and should be put on hold while you deal with the immediate issues at hand.

And when I say "choose happiness" I don't mean to cover over or stuff your feelings. Emotions are always there for a reason. Sometimes it is easy to move through them (revisit "flow-stoppers" in chapter five), but sometimes we're faced with emotional issues that require deeper processing or even professional help to heal.

Setting intentions like these can help:

I intend to feel my emotions freely and fully.

I intend to choose happiness as much as possible.

I intend to be clear about how to deal with my emotions.

I intend to be guided to the resources and practitioners that are most beneficial to me in my emotional healing.

HOW DO YOU FEEL HAPPY WHEN YOU'RE JUST NOT?

We all know that it's sometimes hard to sustain feelings of happiness. Sometimes we just get into a funk and happy seems light-years away. Luckily there are techniques to help get your happy back.

Try one (or more) of these the next time you need a little "getting happy" help:

1. **Get into nature.** Nature is restorative. You don't need to *try*. You don't need to *struggle*. You just need to open yourself to it. Go for a walk, a hike, or a bike ride. Go to the park, look at the stars, walk barefoot in the grass or just sit under a tree and allow Mother Earth to help you to reset.

2. **Count your blessings.** Everyone gets into places of lethargy or self-pity. Some of us have even greater challenges of victimhood, depression or cynicism. But if you honestly sit in gratitude you *will* be lifted to

a higher resonance. It's quick. It's easy. You can do it anywhere. Make a list (in your head or written out) of all you are grateful for, and feel your resonance shift.

3. **Listen to music.** Music transcends. It uplifts. It makes you happy and actually releases dopamine, a feel-good chemical, into your brain. It seems to suspend time, allowing you to reboot and start all over again.

4. **Be inspired.** There is nothing that makes us happier than truth. The fact that we create our own reality gives us hope that if something isn't right with our world, it can change. It isn't something outside of us that will change it...it is *us*.

   So when you find yourself less than happy, read an inspiring book, do a reconnecting meditation, or visit an inspirational web page. Pay attention to what you find inspiring so you can go back to it time and again.

5. **Find something happy to do.** We all have things we do that make us happy— being with those we love, reading, hiking, watching a funny movie or indulging in a much-loved hobby. Treat yourself, not just when you feel bad, but also when you feel good. You really can't be too happy.

6. **Remember it is a choice.** Choose. In every moment think..."*I intend to feel happy.*"

7. **Ask your unseen friends to help you to stay happy.**
   You will learn more about how to do this in chapter eleven.

Another way to move gently into happiness is to:

BE FULLY PRESENT

There is something to be said for mindfulness. What I love the most is that it helps you to stay happy.

If you focus on the past, rethinking, regretting, reliving, you generally aren't happy. You either regret something that happened, or you're longing for something you no longer have.

If you focus on the future, wondering, fearing, anticipating or simply planning, you aren't happy either. And you're missing out on the gift of being here *now*.

Of course there are exceptions to that rule, such as writing your intentions, being excited about your day and other reasons to think about the future with joy. But if you focus on the future habitually, you tend to lose the joy of the present. And since it's our intention to flow beautiful energy as much as we possibly can (it *is* your intention, right?) it would be a really fine idea to practice mindfulness.

I've discovered that with mindfulness, everything is much more enjoyable. Mindfully doing the dishes, taking out the trash or meeting a friend for lunch...it doesn't matter what it is, the experience is better.

I have a favorite mindfulness technique I call **Narrowing Your Focus**. I like to use this technique when I'm overwhelmed by a huge job, or I have too much to do and not enough time, or when I'm feeling pressured by all the things I have to do in the future.

All I do is to remind myself to focus on one little piece at a time, and to be fully and totally present with that piece. Even though I may want to clean the whole house, I force myself to focus on straightening the *one* closet. Even though I may have an entire book to write, I focus on *one* sentence. Even though I may want to complete a five mile run, finish a long list of errands and then meet my friends for lunch, I force myself to stay focused on only the immediate present and pay as much attention to *that* as possible. I bring my attention back to the here and now and feel the warm breeze on my face and the earth under my feet and hear the sounds of the birds singing in the trees.

It's not fancy. It's not complicated. But it works. I narrow my focus and the feeling of overwhelm goes way. And I can again choose to be *happy*.

THE MOST IMPORTANT
CHOICE OF MY LIFE

There was a time when I didn't think I had anything to be "happy" about. My divorce was final. My house was in foreclosure. My children moved in with their father and he then moved them across the country. I had no income. I had no job. I had nowhere to live. My one remaining parent had just died. Actually, there was a lot to be "unhappy" about!

I didn't know how to turn my life around, but there was one thing I *did* know for sure:

I was sick and tired of feeling unhappy.

I was tired of feeling scared. I was tired of feeling betrayed. I was tired of feeling broke. I was tired of feeling hopeless. I was tired of feeling helpless.

It was then it hit me. No one was *making* me feel that way. And if no one was *making* me feel that way, I could *choose* another way to feel.

I *chose* happy. *"No matter what happens in my reality,"* I thought, *"I'm not sacrificing my happiness."* I decided, then and there, that I'd rather be a happy bag lady than an unhappy anything else.

And I made my happiness my number one highest priority.

I realized that I had been choosing "bad" feelings almost as a penance for my "bad" reality. As if worrying, lamenting, and fearing would somehow help the situation. Actually, it was the polar opposite. My bad feelings were only making my reality worse.

And the thing is, I *knew* better. I *knew* how reality worked. But I'd been caught in a negative spiral and it wasn't until everything fell apart that I allowed myself to make the choice of *happiness*, above all else. Who cares *when* you make the choice, I figured, as long as you make it.

From then on, I no longer waited for a certain reality to make me happy. I was happy for no reason at all.

And of course, the most amazing thing happened...my reality began to turn around. Yes, I began dreaming again, and yes, I began to flow energy again, and it wasn't the happiness alone that shifted my world. But the happiness sure *helped*.

AND FOR EVEN FASTER CHANGE—FEEL AS IF YOU HAVE THE DREAM...

You practiced feeling as if you already have the dream in the technique, **A Day in the Day of the Dream**. Now it's time to incorporate that feeling into your life 24/7. You will give your dream a huge, wonderful boost of juicy, love-filled flow if you can hold the joy and *feel as if you have that dream* all day, every day.

But if I had my dream now wouldn't my life be different? Couldn't I spend any amount of money I wanted? Wouldn't I be living a totally different life?

Probably. Again, I'm not suggesting you max out your credit cards or put your house on the market. I *am* suggesting you feel *emotionally* as if you have the dream now.

This can also be a really fun mental exercise that you can take into your world. For example:

Go shopping in a store you love. Look around at all the items you want to buy. And say to yourself, *"I can afford everything in this store. My money is not liquid yet, it is still on its way to becoming liquid, but I have it. And as soon as it is liquid, anything and everything in this store can be mine."*

Of course this technique will only work if you can really *feel* the joy of having enough money to buy anything you want in the store. Practice it. The better you get at it, the better it will work. Many see this as "just an exercise"...but I'm telling you, it may be the single most powerful technique you will *ever* do to manifest your dream.

FEELING "AS IF I HAVE THE DREAM" IS MY FAVORITE TECHNIQUE

No one can step into the future without practice. You just can't do it. That future "you" is not *you* yet. You need to practice being who you will become.

But I find that the more I do this, the more my image of myself, my beliefs about myself, and the expectation I have of what my life is and is going to be, shifts.

This practice gives me a chance to "try on" new realities. If I can't imagine something, I know I probably have a belief that says I can't have it. So I go back and change that belief.

If fear comes up, I know I must have a belief that the dream will come with a consequence I don't like. So I change that.

Aside from this being a great tool to discover more about how you see yourself in the dream, it is loads of fun and a great way to flow energy towards your desire.

This does not need to be a formal meditation or exercise. You can do it almost any time—while you are driving to work, in the shower, doing dishes, whatever you are doing...just pretend (emotionally) you *have* the life you want *now*.

If you get good at this, it can be so much fun you won't even mind that you *don't* have the dream yet! And that is exactly, emotionally, where you want to be!

LIFE-ALTERING TAKE AWAYS

Read these slowly. Meditate on them or sit and contemplate them. Let them in. Let them change you.

+ We have *thoughts* all day every day and we have *emotions* with those thoughts. And some of them aren't pretty. And if they're not pretty, they are stealing your dream.

+ If you focus on the past, rethinking, regretting, reliving, you generally aren't happy. You either regret something that happened, or you're longing for something you no longer have. If you focus on the future, wondering, fearing, anticipating, or simply planning, you aren't happy either. And you are missing out on the gift of being here *now*.

+ If you follow The Map you *will* get your dream. But The Map is not just a method to manifest your dreams. The Map is a *way of life*.

+ Don't wait until you have your dream. Honestly, your dream won't give it to you anyway. Be happy *now*.

+ No one can step into the future without practice. You just can't do it. That future "you" is not *you* yet. You need to *practice* being who you will become.

YOUR NEXT STEPS

☐ Practice the **Narrowing Your Focus** technique. For one full day take stock every hour and ask yourself if you are focused on one and only one thing. If not, do so. Notice how much more joy you can feel if you are not overwhelmed with a hundred things in your head at one time.

☐ Spend an entire day feeling "as if you have the dream." How do you go about your day differently? Who is the "you" who has the dream? Write the answers to these questions in your journal and keep note of any changes in your world.

☐ Make a list of the things that make you feel happy. Turn to this list when you need to shift your emotions back to happiness.

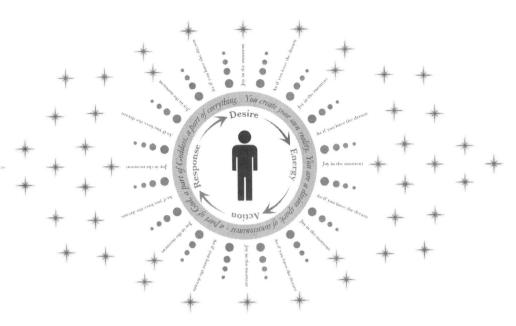

ELEVEN

MAKE ROOM FOR MIRACLES

*"Whenever you really ask for help,
and not just pity, you will always receive it."*

—RANA

Yes, it gets even better than *"you create your own reality and you can learn to do it consciously."* How?

As I've mentioned, you have help available. Lots of it. Tons of it. You need only to ask.

Wait, I thought I needed to take responsibility for my reality... why not just turn it all over to God if there is so much help?

I didn't say they'll do it for you. They will *help* you. God, Goddess, your guides, angels, whomever you ask will be there to help you uncover and discover what stops you from creating the life you long for. They will send energy, information and resources.

AFTER YOU TAKE RESPONSIBILITY

They won't do it for you. You need to do it for yourself. But they will help. However, if you're bound and determined to feel sorry for yourself, play the victim, blame others, blah, blah, blah, their hands are tied. Why?

Because *this is a free will universe.* This is what you ordered.

SO ASK

Every time you are stymied, ask for assistance. If you have trouble finding the root of a creation, ask your unseen friends to show you. If you have a repeating pattern that seems resistant to change, ask them to help you heal it. If you are unclear about how to state something in your intentions, ask them to guide you. If you have difficulty forgiving yourself or others, ask them to help you to forgive. Ask for help in discovering and changing your beliefs.

Whatever it is you desire, ask for help. It can't hurt, right? And it *can* be of tremendous benefit.

Before you read your intentions each morning and night, call upon your unseen friends to help you manifest those intentions easily and elegantly. Such a request might be something like this:

> *"I call upon my higher self, my soul, my spirit and all unseen friends who would love to assist me in the conscious creation of my personal heaven on earth. I ask for your support and assistance in manifesting all of my intentions with ease and elegance, in the perfect timing and with harm to none.*

> *I ask to become aware of any beliefs or habits that stand in my way and that the learning and growing that takes place be both gentle and loving.*

> *I ask for your assistance in feeling my emotions fully as I read these intentions and to help me to recognize the little and big signs that will show the realities*

manifesting in my world.

I ask for your assistance in helping me to manifest a dream even better than my intentions state, and I thank you in advance for your love and support."

This will more easily open the doors for everything you intend to manifest.

YOU CAN ALSO ASK THEM TO HELP YOU TO STAY HAPPY

When I was first learning to consciously create my reality I would slip into feelings of disappointment, depression, impatience and doubt. I *knew* those emotions were not at all in the flow of my dream. Even so, it was sometimes difficult for me to choose another emotion.

I would stop, sit and talk to my higher self. *"Higher self, I want to feel joy right now. I choose joy. Help me feel and stay in that emotion."* And sure enough within a few minutes I was back in my happy place.

YOU WON'T BE PERFECT

Don't expect to be perfect. Forgive yourself when you mess up. It's supposed to be fun, remember?

You are in a *partnership* with your unseen friends. They want to help you, guide you and assist you in lifting your resonance. Your life should be easier as a result of working with them.

And if you don't feel their support, their guidance, their love, ask that they show you in a more direct or clear way.

I ASKED...AND ASKED...AND ASKED...

When I was a newbie at communicating with my unseen friends, I wasn't always sure they were hearing me or answering my requests. Fortunately for me, my higher self and guides didn't seem to take it personally when I continually asked for more clarification.

One of my favorite ways to connect with my unseen friends was to ask for "signs" from them. I was amazed at how easy it was to receive confirmation and direction with this simple request. In one case, it totally changed my life.

In 1990 I was just beginning my final year of a combined JD/ MBA program. I had done well in both programs, and had landed a law clerkship at the end of my first year in law school.

But the previous year had shaken me up. My brother, barely thirty, with four young children, had suffered an industrial accident and, after a series of operations, lost his leg. And my mother, just fifty-six years old, had died of cervical cancer.

I remember sitting in the law library wondering if my mother had led a happy life. Had she followed her bliss? I didn't think she had.

And that got me thinking...*was I following my bliss?* I had spent two years studying law and clerking in a large law firm. Did I love it? Did I even *like* it? The answer hit me hard. I did not.

The truth was petrifying. I had just spent years of my life in graduate school. I was at the top of my class. I had spent countless hours and money we did not have, in order to follow a dream that wasn't even mine. And *now* I figure out that I don't *love* it?

In just one more year I would earn both degrees. Surely I could stick it out for a few short months in order to have these degrees under my belt?

On the other hand, that would be an entire *year* of my *life*. Certainly no amount of time is worth spending on something you do not love?

I was torn. Somewhere deep inside I knew I had to cut my losses and move on. But another part of me thought I was a fool. "*What? Are you crazy?*" that part said.

Then I remembered something...that we have guides assisting us from the other side. Asking *them* seemed like the perfect solution!

At the moment of this epiphany I happened to be at a local country carnival. I was buying a scratch lottery ticket at a fundraiser booth for a preschool.

I held the ticket in my hand, and before scratching off the coating, I mentally said to my guides, *"OK, I need some advice and I need it now. Is it the right decision to quit graduate school? If it is, let me have a winning ticket."*

I took a deep breath, and started scratching. I had won! Two free tickets! OK, not a windfall, but still I had *won* and better yet, I had my answer! I was probably more excited about winning those tickets than anyone had ever been, because now I was free to end the path of corporate law and find my true bliss!

My negative self was quick to chime in, *"Are you kidding me? You really think that means anything? Probably every other ticket wins two tickets. It's how they get you back there to buy more tickets, stupid!"*

I thought, *"What if that's true? I'm going to throw away years of graduate school for a fifty-cent lottery ticket? This is insane!"*

I threw down the tickets, disheartened. And then I thought, *"OK, if that was a sign, I can't just ignore it."*

Again I asked, *"Higher self, I may be having some difficulty understanding your signs. You see, I wasn't sure you sent that one. Will you please send me another sign if indeed, quitting law school is the right thing for me? And make it a bigger sign!"*

Immediately there was an announcement over the loudspeaker, *"Boni Lonnsburry please report to the information booth. Congratulations! You have just won a free* tree *courtesy of the Boy Scouts of America."*

Oh my god! I had my sign! I was relieved, excited, ecstatic and grateful. I could move forward now, certain I was doing the right thing!

My resolve lasted three days. When it came time to actually resign from school I was filled with fear again. What if it were just a coincidence? Was I really going to base my entire future on a *tree*?

I drove to school slowly. Each mile closer filled me with more trepidation. I stopped on the way at a metaphysical bookstore, anxious for any reason to postpone my decision.

As I parked the car and entered the store, I reached out one more time, *"OK higher self. I may be really thick about this, but I need yet another sign if quitting law school is the right decision to make. And please, make this a sign I cannot rationalize my way out of, OK?"*

I took my time in the store, picking out some books both for my children and myself. As I walked to the counter to pay for them, I heard a little voice in my head, *"Make another round of the store...you missed something."*

Did I imagine it? Was this just a postponement tactic? I wasn't sure, but I decided to humor the voice and make another round.

This time I saw it. A little paperback entitled, *A Nation of Lawyers*, by Paul Williams. Odd, I thought, that a metaphysical bookstore would have a book about lawyers.

It was a poetry book. I picked it up and opened the book directly to a page which read:

> *"...the only question worth asking is,*
> *is my heart in the work?*
> *If your heart's not in the work,*
> *Don't argue with it.*
> *Listen to what it tells you.*
> *It will bring you to what you have to do."*

That was the day I quit. And I never looked back.

AND MIRACLES *DO* HAPPEN

Believe it or not, having all that help at your fingertips isn't even the miraculous part. Miracles are *real*. It's a miracle when our unseen friends give us *even more* than we've asked for! Yep, that's right! Miracles occur when we are given the help, realities, insights and signs that we didn't ask for, didn't expect and sometimes can't even imagine!

Now, I have no idea how they can pull off these miracles in a free will universe where we must ask for help to allow them in. I'm just grateful it's so.

And while you can't *cause* miracles to happen, you *can* increase the likelihood of miracles in your world. How?

Be open to them. Expect them to happen. And be grateful for them when they do show up.

LIFE-ALTERING TAKE AWAYS

Read these slowly. Meditate on them or sit and contemplate them. Let them in. Let them change you.

+ Every time you are stymied, ask for assistance. If you have trouble finding the root of a creation, ask your unseen friends to show you. If you have a repeating pattern that seems resistant to change, ask them to help you heal it. If you are unclear about how to state something in your intentions, ask them to guide you. If you have difficulty forgiving yourself or others, ask them to help you to forgive. Ask for help in discovering and changing your beliefs. Whatever your desire, ask for help. It can't hurt, right? And it *can* be of tremendous benefit.

+ Don't expect to be perfect. Forgive yourself when you mess up. It's supposed to be fun, remember? You are in a *partnership* with your unseen friends. They want to help you, guide you and assist you in lifting your resonance. Your life should be easier as a result of working with them.

+ Miracles occur when we are given the help, realities, insights and signs that we didn't ask for, didn't expect and sometimes can't even imagine!

YOUR NEXT STEPS

☐ Think about the times in your life when you knew you were guided, assisted and loved by your unseen friends. Thank them for this.

☐ Ask. In your own words. Ask your higher self and other unseen friends to help you, guide you and show themselves to you, in gentle and loving ways.

☐ Use meditation as a way to meet and begin to know your higher self. Talk with your higher self about your dreams, your passions and your joys. Let your higher self talk to you about its dreams for *you*.

TWELVE

CHANGING YOUR LIFE

*"You are never given a wish without
also being given the power to make it true.
You may have to work for it, however."*

—RICHARD BACH

I hope you are beginning to realize this book is not just another "how to" book. It is a threshold to an entirely new way of *looking at, living in* and *reacting to* your world. It is my knowing that once you've fully let this book into your heart and soul, you will never be the same.

That said, I fully believe that knowledge is power, but only if you *act* upon that knowledge. The more effort you put into consciously creating your reality, the more your life will change. However *how* you go about creating your dream life is up to you. There is no *right* way to approach conscious creation and no *wrong* way. It is less about the specifics of *what* you do, and more about how it makes you *feel*.

You will know you are on the right track if you are motivated, excited, having fun and if your life is changing for the better.

You will find that sometimes it feels right to move quickly, other times it will feel right to slow the pace down. Slowing down gives you time to integrate the changes you've made in yourself and your world, so allow yourself those pauses. Just don't slip from "pause" to "stop."

And for those of you who would like even more guidance, I include some suggestions for:

1. Creating new dreams
2. Staying in the magic day to day

3. Troubleshooting your reality
4. Suggestions for support

CREATING A NEW DREAM

New dreams require more time and energy than sustaining an ongoing dream. My suggestion is to spend thirty minutes at a time on your new dreams. I have prepared seven sample "creation sessions" to use for guidance. These sessions are for guidance purposes only. Feel free to mix and match techniques in the way that feels right to you.

You could do one of these sample sessions each day for seven days. Or, if you want to do two or three sessions in a day, that is fine (but give yourself a break between them). If you want to do a session a week, that is fine too.

You have a cadence of growth that is perfect for you at any given moment in time. Trust it. Above all else, though, have fun. It really is about the journey.

BEFORE YOU BEGIN:

☐ Read this book at least once in its entirety.

☐ Write your intentions *(chapter four)* and date them. Every time you update your intentions save a new copy with the current date.

SUGGESTED CREATION SESSIONS:

Session One: Prepare your space. Turn off your phone and computer. Become quiet and begin:

☐ Call in your higher self with the **Invitation to Assist** *(appendix c)*.

☐ Do the **Blending with Your Higher Self** technique *(chapter three)*. Make a note in your journal about this experience.

☐ Choose an area of your life that will be your primary dream for the next week. *(This does not mean you shouldn't do techniques for other areas. You will just give this area more attention than others.)*

☐ Re-read your intentions for the primary dream. Assess whether you would like to add to them or change them in any way. Make sure they fully state what you would like to create.

☐ Do the **Igniting Your Intentions** technique *(chapter seven)*. Make a note in your journal when you have done this.

☐ Do the **Closing with Gratitude** technique *(appendix c)*.

The rest of the day:

☐ Stay in joy, as much as you possibly can *(chapter ten)*.

Session Two: Prepare your space. Turn off your phone and computer. Become quiet and begin:

☐ Call in your higher self with the **Invitation to Assist** *(appendix c)*.

☐ Read your intentions, feeling as much excitement as possible.

☐ Sit quietly and re-visit the section on "flow-stoppers" *(chapter five)*. Think about whether you tend to habitually feel any of these emotions, especially around your primary dream. Make a note of this in your journal.

☐ Do the **A Day in the Day of the Dream** technique *(chapter seven)*.

☐ Reflect on the past twenty-four hours and your ability to remain in a state of joy. On a scale of one to ten (ten being the most joyful), how would you rate yourself? Make note in your journal.

☐ Think about the past few days. What signs have you received that indicate you are moving towards

manifesting your dream *(chapter nine)?* Make
note in your journal.

☐ Do the **Closing with Gratitude** technique
(appendix c).

The rest of the day:

☐ Focus on being present today *(chapter ten).* Notice
which thoughts take you away from the present
moment and make note in your journal.

Session Three: Prepare your space. Turn off your phone and
computer. Become quiet and begin:

☐ Call in your higher self with the **Invitation to
Assist** *(appendix c).*

☐ Read your intentions, feeling as much excitement
as possible. Any trouble feeling excited? Maybe
you don't fully *believe* it is possible, or possible for
you?

☐ Visit your child self, your adolescent self and your
young adult self in a visualization *(chapter five).*
Tell them what you are planning to create (the primary dream). Ask them how they feel about that.
Make a note in your journal.

☐ Read the **Letter from Your Future Self** or write your own *(appendix b)*. Imagine being there... imagine being this person. How are they different from you, especially emotionally? How do they move through their day? How easily do they laugh, play and have fun? Make a note in your journal.

☐ Reflect on the past twenty-four hours and your ability to stay in the present moment. On a scale of one to ten (ten being the most present), how would you rate yourself? Make note in your journal.

☐ Think about the past few days. What signs have you received that indicate you are moving towards manifesting your dream *(chapter nine)*? Make note in your journal.

☐ Do the **Closing with Gratitude** technique *(appendix c)*.

The rest of the day:

☐ Begin to act as if you already had the dream (use the experience of reflecting on your future self today as inspiration).

Session Four: Prepare your space. Turn off your phone and computer. Become quiet and begin:

☐ Call in your higher self with the **Invitation to Assist** *(appendix c)*.

☐ Read your intentions, feeling as much excitement as possible.

☐ Think about your primary dream—the one you are focused on creating right now. In your journal, write about your history on this subject, i.e. your history with men/women if your primary dream has to do with a relationship, your history with money, or health, or career, etc.

☐ Has anything happened in your past around this issue, that you still feel strong emotion about? If yes, write a "Hate Letter"—not to give to anyone but to release the emotion *(chapter six)*.

☐ Do the **Making the Movie Real** technique *(chapter seven)*.

☐ Reflect on the past twenty-four hours as to how well you held the resonance of having the dream. On a scale of one to ten (ten being that you felt all day as if you really did have the dream), how would you rate yourself? Make note in your journal.

☐ Think about the past few days. What signs have you received that indicate you are moving towards

manifesting your dream *(chapter nine)*? Make note in your journal.

☐ Do the **Closing with Gratitude** technique *(appendix c).*

The rest of the day:

☐ Stay happy, be present in the moment, as if you had the dream.

Session Five: Prepare your space. Turn off your phone and computer. Become quiet and begin:

☐ Call in your higher self with the **Invitation to Assist** *(appendix c).*

☐ Read your intentions, feeling as much excitement as possible.

☐ Visualize sitting with your negative self. Tell it what you intend to create in the area of your primary dream. Let it tell you how impossible that is. How idiotic. How stupid. How you will fail. What a ridiculous idea that is. Let it rant and rave and when they finally pause, ask it if it is complete. It will not be. Let it tear into you about other areas of your life as well. Let it drone on and on, dumping all of its venom. And when it is complete, call your

higher self to take your negative self away for healing. Feel the freedom *(chapter five)*.

☐ Do the **Grateful for "Now and Then"** technique *(chapter seven)*.

☐ How did you do yesterday with staying in joy, in
the moment, as if you had the dream? Make note
in your journal.

☐ Think about the past few days. What signs have
you received that indicate you are moving towards
manifesting your dream *(chapter nine)*? Make
note in your journal.

☐ Do the **Closing with Gratitude** technique
(appendix c).

The rest of the day:

☐ Don't forget: stay happy, be present in the moment,
as if you had the dream.

Session Six: Prepare your space. Turn off your phone and
computer. Become quiet and begin:

☐ Call in your higher self with the **Invitation to
Assist** *(appendix c)*.

☐ Read your intentions, feeling as much excitement as possible. Do any of your intentions need to be eliminated, changed or strengthened? If yes, do so now.

☐ Go over your notes from your time with your child, adolescent and young adult. Also go over your notes regarding the history of the area of your primary dream *(session four)*. Make a list of beliefs that are standing in your way of creating this dream and label them level one, two or three. Write the new beliefs *(chapter six)*.

☐ Write out an action plan for your primary dream *(chapter eight)*. What action on that list will you take this week? Make a note.

☐ How are you doing at staying in the moment, staying in joy and feeling as if you already have the dream? Make a note.

☐ Think about the past few days. What signs have you received that indicate you are moving towards manifesting your dream *(chapter nine)*? Make note in your journal.

☐ Do the **Closing with Gratitude** technique *(appendix c)*.

The rest of the day:

☐ It should be getting a bit easier now...to stay present, in joy, and to feel as if the dream has already happened.

Session Seven: Prepare your space. Turn off your phone and computer. Become quiet and begin:

☐ Call in your higher self with the **Invitation to Assist** *(appendix c).*

☐ Read your intentions, feeling as much excitement as possible.

☐ Do the **Your Nurturing Universe** technique *(chapter three).*

☐ Change the beliefs you prepared last session *(chapter six).* Write out the new beliefs and post them in your bathroom, bedroom or kitchen so you can read them whenever you see them (with joy, gratitude and excitement please!).

☐ Make a list of things that will help you stay in joy should you slip out temporarily *(chapter eleven).*

☐ Think about the past few days. What signs have you received that indicate you are moving towards

manifesting your dream *(chapter nine)*? Make note in your journal.

☐ Do the **Closing with Gratitude** technique *(appendix c)*.

The rest of the day:

☐ You know what to do...

STAYING IN THE MAGIC DAY TO DAY

Here are some suggestions to keep in mind on a day-to-day basis, whether you are working on a new dream or simply sustaining the dream life you currently have.

> *Remember you are creating it all, consciously or not. (Yeah, maybe you think I've beat this one to death, but until you are* living *this 24/7, my work is not done!)*

> *Rate yourself today: According to the spiritual teacher Lazaris, "There are two focuses, however, that are part of every lifetime we have:*
> *1. Learning to Have Fun and*
> *2. Learning to Consciously Create Success"*[1]
> *How are you doing on these fronts?*

---

1   Interviews: Book II (out of print). More information available at: www.lazaris.com

Give yourself the gift of daily intimacy with yourself. Spend fifteen to thirty minutes each day alone, quietly staring out a window. Let your mind wander. Allow ideas, feelings and direction to surface.

Get to know yourself better. Explore the Enneagram, numerology, dreams or astrology as a means to better understand yourself and others.

Remember who you are: Divine. Gifted. Unique. With talents like no one else on the planet.

Appreciate what you have "let" happen or "made" happen in your world. Spend five minutes a day feeling truly grateful.

Design a "self-love date" with yourself weekly or monthly. Plan two hours and do something you absolutely adore. Do it and enjoy (sans guilt)!

Give your intentions some lovin' —post 'em with this list and read them with joy and excitement often!

Practice giving yourself the freedom to do what excites you, every minute you can.

Get to know your unseen friends. They are real. They have personalities. They can be fun (and unbelievably helpful!).

Don't wait for your dreams to manifest before you are happy. Be happy now.

Remember everything is you and everything is a part of the Divine. Treat yourself, others and the planet accordingly.

TROUBLESHOOTING YOUR REALITY

As previously mentioned, you won't be perfect at this. And sometimes it will seem as though your reality has absolutely no correlation with *you* whatsoever. If you are having challenges with consciously creating your reality, run through this checklist and find out why:

☐ **What have you been thinking and feeling (on a day to day basis) around this issue?**

Nine times out of ten people think about what they *don't* want rather than what they *do* (i.e. they are worrying about something happening or not happening which pushes away the thing they desire). It takes some time and discipline to steer your mind in the direction of your dreams all day, every day.

☐ **Are you clear about what you *do* want?** Are your intentions crystal clear about all aspects of the thing you desire? If not, clarify them. If you are unsure, find someone to work with you on this issue.

☐ **Have you stopped flowing negative energy?** Go back to chapter five and take a look at whether you have been stopping the flow with one of the "flow-stopper" emotions.

☐ **Have you been proactively flowing energy?** Have you been doing regular (at minimum once a week) techniques to flow positive energy towards your dream?

☐ **Have you taken inspired action?** If not, why not? Revisit chapter eight.

☐ **Have you been patient enough to allow the new dream to manifest?** Bigger dreams take longer. Although there are no absolute time tables to consult, with practice you will begin to get a *feel* for where you are in the manifestation process.

☐ **Have you been watching the "signs"?** *All* dreams respond with signs when a powerful technique is implemented. But you won't see them if you aren't looking.

☐ **Is there something/someone you need to forgive?** If so, release your emotions. Forgive or get some help in forgiving. Sometimes professional help is appropriate and a godsend. Intend to forgive and/or seek the assistance. And accept the help.

☐ **Take a look at your beliefs.** If you don't find the reason for the mis-creation anywhere else, delve deeply into *your beliefs*. Revisit chapters five and six.

☐ **What's that?** You are *certain* none of these suggestions apply to you? Then, my friend, I suggest professional assistance. Sometimes (very, very rarely) there is a deep-rooted cause for the energies we flow. But there is always, repeat, *always* a reason for every reality. *No one* is an exception to the truth that we create our own reality. Ask to be guided to the perfect person to help you through this dark place.

SUGGESTIONS FOR SUPPORT

I have had a heck of a lot of support in creating my "dream life." Dozens, perhaps hundreds, perhaps even thousands of people and entities have joined me on my quest to build a life I love. None of them have done it *for* me. But they assisted. And the more wholehearted my quest, the more assistance I received.

I have already covered requesting support from your unseen friends. However I'm certain some of you may want to form support "groups" to discuss and implement this information with each other.

Finding like-minded people to talk to about these concepts can be extremely beneficial, especially if you are new to the idea of conscious creation. It is important that a protocol is followed, however, so that the group doesn't become side-tracked by gossip or complaining.

Therefore, I suggest these guidelines for implementing "**The Map**" **Support Groups:**

CLARIFY INTENTIONS

Intentions could be those below or similar intentions in your own words:

We intend that this group draws to it the assistance of the unseen friends of all members as well as the light beings in support of this work as a whole.

We intend that this group operates with the highest integrity and character possible.

We intend that this group holds the highest level of light, love and support possible for ourselves and each other.

We intend that this group aids its members in discovering deeper levels of "who we really are" and in consciously creating lives we love.

We intend that the growth and learning in this group is (as much as is possible) easy, elegant and fun.

We intend to adhere to the guidelines of the group out of love and respect for ourselves and each other.

CHOOSE DEFINITIONS OF GROUP

☐ Choose the number of members (minimum and maximum).

☐ Decide where to meet (if not a public venue then switching homes is ideal).

☐ Decide how often to meet (weekly or monthly).

☐ Choose your facilitator (rotate between all those willing).

SUGGESTED MEETING GUIDELINES

☐ Small talk shall be limited to before and after the meeting.

☐ There shall be no complaining, lamenting or self-pity during the meeting hours. This energy is not conducive to fun, abundant and joyous realities.

☐ A timer shall be used to time those speaking to keep the meeting on task and allow all a turn. Someone shall be appointed "time keeper" for each meeting (ideally this person changes from meeting to meeting).

☐ Intentions should be requested from all who participate. Those who do not "have time" to write intentions should not be allowed entry. This is not to be mean or to single them out, but the group should be limited to those serious about creating their realities.

SUGGESTED FORMAT

☐ Read the "Group" intentions.

☐ Read all intentions for new people to the group, and overall and immediate intentions along with any changed intentions for ongoing members. Affirm aloud that the unread intentions are included.

☐ Successes and/or signs announced (each in turn).

☐ Read one to two page(s) of this book per person (can be related to the group technique below).

☐ Group technique (from the book).

☐ Individual "case study." One person comes prepared to speak about their success or troubleshoot a difficult manifestation. This person should bring and read their:

- Intentions (around this topic)
- The beliefs they have changed
- The techniques they have completed
- The actions they have taken
- The signs they have received

If troubleshooting, others should listen for other beliefs/techniques/ideas around the topic being discussed and share those suggestions with the individual.

☐ Read closing statement (this or something similar): *We give thanks for everyone in attendance today that assisted in our growth and intention to consciously create lives we love. We give thanks for the unseen friends who have assisted us tonight/today. We ask that they continue to support us throughout the coming week/month in consciously creating realities of ease, elegance, love, joy, prosperity, abundance, success, freedom and fun.*

For more information on "The Map" Support Groups visit www.livealifeyoulove.com

IN CLOSING

Thank you, fellow creator, for reading this book, for your open-mindedness and your searching heart. You are a courageous pioneer, opening to a world of possibilities you cannot even imagine right now.

Be gentle with yourself. Nurture the new "you" who is being birthed. As with an infant, be careful of what and who you expose this new life to. Surround yourself, as much as possible, with people who support you, respect you and honor your path.

Let me know when your life begins to reflect who you really are. I would love to hear from you. Email your successes, questions and comments to BoniLonnsburry@livealifeyoulove.com

It has been a joy.

With love,

THE MAP INDEX

adolescent self, 114, 117, 121, 126, 127, 132-135, 141, 143, 145, 170, 193, 201, 279, 322, 327

aging, regression, 7, In

assistance, *see unseen friends*

beliefs, 113, 116-121, 123, 126-129, 132-135, 141, 142, 147-201, 209, 217-218, 222-224, 272-273, 275, 282, 286, 327-328, 333, 337

beliefs, core 50, 164-165, 179, 190-197, 201

beliefs, level one, 181-182

beliefs, level two, 182-191, 194, 201

beliefs, level three, 190-197, 201

blame, 122

blame, antidote, 122

Building of Beliefs, 189, 196

checklist, 105, 343

child self, 126-133, 135, 141, 143, 145, 170, 193, 201, 279, 322, 327

conscious creation, 13, 15, 25, 31, 40, 42, 44, 53, 62, 126, 143, 254, 267, 269, 277-278, 285

conscious mind, 63, 171-173

control, 116

control, antidote, 116-117

cynicism, 21

desire, 15, 63-65, 69, 74, 88, 103, 104, 108, 113, 142, 143-144

disappointment, 120, 236

disappointment, antidote, 121-122

doubt, 112

doubt, antidote, 112-113

emotions, 15, 64, 108-110, 127, 136, 143, 145, *see also feeling state*

emotions, postive, 108-109, 143, 215, 233, 250

entitlement, 122

entitlement, antidote, 123

fear, 19, 113

fear, antidote, 114-115

feeling state, 15, 16, 25, 70, 104, 237, *see also emotions*

flowing energy, 34-35, 37, 40, 108-110, 112, 126, 130, 132, 143-144, 204, 213, 215-216, 225, 227, 254, 257-269,

271-273, 275-276, 281-283, 285, 290, 292-293, 296, 299, 301, 321, 332-333

Flow-stoppers, 110-126
blame, 122
control, 116-117
disappointment, 120-122
doubt, 112-113
entitlement, 122-123
fear, 113-115
guilt, 123-124
impatience, 117-119
jealousy, 124-125
judgment, 119-120
martyrdom, 115
shame, 125-126
self-pity, 111

forgiveness, 49, 59, 67, 152, 168, 201, 308, 315, 332
free will, 13, 28, 41, 306, 314
future self, 14, 355, 357

gratitude list, 111
God-being, 28, 48, 49, 60
guilt, 123-124
guilt, antidote, 124
guides, *see unseen friends*

happiness, 8, 291-299, 302-303, 308, 310
hate letter, 150-151, 324

higher self, 41, 50, 51, 55, 59, 98, 139, 145, 307-312, 316, 359-360

impatience, 117-118, 332
impatience, antidote 118-119
intentions, 63-105, 204-205, 219, 347-354
intentions, overall, 70
intentions, core, 71-79, 81
intentions, immediate, 79-81
intentions, closing request, 81
intentions, tips, 82-88

jealousy, 124
jealousy, antidote, 124-125
judgment, 119
judgment, antidote, 119-120
journal, creation, 26
journal, success, 26
joy, in, 233, 237-238, 240, 242-244, 250, 308, 316

law of attraction, 292
Lazaris, Acknowledgments, 125, 127, 140
letting go, 216-227

Map, the, 3-8, 41, 42, 43, 104
martyrdom, 115
martyrdom, antidote, 115
mindfulness, 296-297

negative self, 137-142, 144-145, 270, 278-282, 325

patience, 275-276, 286

present moment, 39, 40

regret, 49, 59
resistance, 19
response, 38, 39, 253-287
responsibility, 14, 25, 270, 277-278, 306

self image, 278-284
self-pity, 111
self-pity, antidote, 111
shame, 125
shame, antidote, 125-126
signs, 254-287
signs, positive and negative, 271-275
subconscious mind 35, 63, 119-120, 142, 172-174, 178, 182, 188, 194-197, 200
support groups, 333-337

techniques
A Day in the Day of the Dream, 205-209, 287, 299, 321
Blending with Your Higher Self, 55, 56, 60, 320
Closing with Gratitude, 320, 322-323, 325-328, 359-360
Grateful for Now and Then, 210-213, 287, 326
Igniting Intentions, 204-205, 320
Invitation to Assist, 320-322, 324-326, 359-260
Letter from Your Future Self, 323, 355-357
Make the Movie Real, 209-210, 287, 324
Narrow Your Focus, 297
Pre-sleep Request, 55, 60
Your Nurturing Universe, 56, 57, 58, 60

taking action, 35, 37, 38, 230-251
time lag, 31, 44
troubleshooting, 319, 331-333, 337
trust, 214-219, 223, 227

unseen friends, 19, 41, 50, 51, 52, 53, 54, 59, 81, 98, 99, 188, 194-195, 311-312, 314-315, 354
universal law, 22

young adult self, 126, 135-137, 141, 143, 145, 170, 193, 201, 322, 327

APPENDIX A

BUILDING A DREAM FROM THE ASHES

Sometimes we are so mired in a life we *dislike*, we have a hard time imagining a life we *love*. When that happens, we must use what we don't like as a starting point to build a dream. This checklist will guide you in that process.

☐ **Make a list of what you dislike in your life**
  Such as:
  - I don't have enough money to live the way I want to live
  - I don't like my job
  - My partner and I fight a lot
  - The dog next door barks all night long

- I don't like my house

☐ **Make a list** of what you dislike about yourself
  Such as:
  - I am not very patient
  - I am depressed that my life isn't going well
  - I am fat
  - I zone out and spend my time on the computer or watching TV
  - I can't seem to find my passion

☐ **Combine** the two lists into one list
  Such as:
  - I don't have enough money to live the way I want to live
  - I don't like my job
  - My partner and I fight a lot
  - The dog next door barks all night long
  - I don't like my house
  - I am not very patient
  - I am depressed that my life isn't going well
  - I am fat
  - I zone out and spend my time on the computer or watching TV
  - I can't seem to find my passion

☐ **Go back and elaborate** on the things that are vague
  Such as:
  - I don't have enough money to live the way I

want to live

- o I want to buy a nicer car
- o My furniture is old and ragged
- o I would like to travel to foreign countries
- o I would like to eat in a nice restaurant once a week
- o I would like help cleaning my house once a month
- o I would like some new clothes

· I don't like my job

- o It is monotonous
- o It doesn't pay well
- o My boss is not fun to work for
- o It is not very creative

· My partner and I fight a lot

- o Mostly about money
- o Sometimes about his mother

· The dog next door barks all night long

- o (Not much to elaborate on here)

· I don't love my home

- o See raggedy furniture (above)
- o See dog barking (above)
- o It is cramped—we need more space
- o It is not in a great neighborhood

· I am not very patient

- o (Yes, I would like my life changed NOW.)

· I am depressed that my life isn't going well (See above—all of above!)

- I am fat
  - o Well, maybe fat is exaggerating, but I could lose five or ten
  - o I could definitely tone up
- I zone out and spend my time on the computer or watching TV
  - o (Who would blame me, right? See above—sigh.)
- I can't seem to find my passion
  - o (No surprise, eh?)

☐ **Copy that list and turn the dislikes into "wants"** and make them positive (for example, instead of "I want to stop fighting with my partner" write, "I want to get along well with my partner").

Such as:

- I want enough money to live the way I want to live
- I want to have a nicer car
- I want new furniture
- I want to travel to foreign countries
- I want to eat in a nice restaurant once a week
- I want help cleaning my house once a month
- I want some new clothes
- I want to like my job
- I want a job that is exciting
- I want a job that pays well
- I want a job with a boss who is fun to work for
- I want a job that is very creative

- I want to get along well with my partner
- I want to make peace around my partner's mother
- I want to have quiet and peaceful nights
- I want to love my home
- I want a home that is spacious
- I want a home in a great neighborhood
- I want to be patient
- I want to be happy that my life is going better
- I want to be thin
- I want to be toned
- I want to be conscious, awake and clear about how I spend my time
- I want to feel passionate about my life

☐ **Change the word "want" to "intend"** and read through the intentions, tweaking them here and there. Work with them to make them feel expansive, exciting and in alignment with what you really desire.

Such as:

- I intend to have enough money to live the way I want to live
- I intend to have a nicer car
- I intend to have new furniture
- I intend to travel to foreign countries
- I intend to eat in a nice restaurant once a week
- I intend to have help cleaning my house once a month
- I intend to have new clothes

- I intend to like my job
- I intend to have a job that is exciting
- I intend to have a job that pays well
- I intend to have a job with a boss who is fun to work for
- I intend to work at a job that is very creative
- I intend to get along well with my partner
- I intend to make peace around my partner's mother
- I intend to have quiet and peaceful nights
- I intend to love my home
- I intend to live in a home that is spacious
- I intend to live in a home in a great neighborhood
- I intend to be patient
- I intend to be happy
- I intend to be thin
- I intend to be toned
- I intend to be conscious and awake and intentional about how I spend my time
- I intend to feel passionate about my life

☐ **Categorize your list of intentions** and add headings
Such as:

- **Life Partnership Intentions:**
  - o I intend to get along well with my partner

- **Other Relationships Intentions:**
  - o I intend to make peace around my partner's mother

- **Work Intentions:**
  - o I intend to like my job
  - o I intend to have a job that is exciting
  - o I intend to have a job that pays well
  - o I intend to have a job with a boss who is fun to work for
  - o I intend to have a job that is very creative

- **Physical Body Intentions:**
  - o I intend to be thin
  - o I intend to be toned

- **Physical Surroundings Intentions:**
  - o I intend to have quiet and peaceful nights
  - o I intend to love my home
  - o I intend to live in a home that is spacious
  - o I intend to live in a home in a great neighborhood

- **Mental and Emotional Intentions:**
  - o I intend to be patient
  - o I intend to be happy
  - o I intend to be conscious and awake and clear about how I spend my time
  - o I intend to feel passionate about my life

- **Financial Intentions:**
  - o I intend to have enough money to live the way I want to live

- **Lifestyle Intentions:**
  - o I intend to have a nice car
  - o I intend to have new furniture
  - o I intend to travel to foreign countries
  - o I intend to eat in a nice restaurant once a week
  - o I intend to have help cleaning my house once a month
  - o I intend to create the ability to buy new clothes whenever I want

☐ **Go back to the list of intentions. Add other headings** that you haven't yet included

Such as:
- Spiritual intentions
- Intentions for play
- Creative intentions
- Intentions for the Earth and Humanity
- Cosmic Intentions
- Intentions for my children
- Intentions for my pets
- Intentions for my country
- Intentions for my community
- Intentions for a particular project (creative project, work project, home project, training

for something...)

☐ **Add additional intentions** to the list (revisit the sample intentions in chapter four for more inspiration)

☐ **Add an "Overall Intention"** category and write that intention

    Such as:

- **Overall Intention:** I intend to experience greater and greater levels of empowerment, joy, fun, love, compassion, creativity and connectedness to "All That Is."

☐ **Add a category of "Immediate Intentions"** and put the intentions that are the most important to you right now on that list.

    Such as:

- **Immediate Intentions:**
  - o I intend to buy a new car that is cute, sporty, affordable, dependable and fun to drive, in perfect timing with harm to none.
  - o I intend to find a new job that pays well, is exciting and close to home with flexible hours. I intend to work with people who are fun and team players.

☐ **Expand your intentions past how they will look when they will manifest, to how they will feel when they**

manifest (for all but immediate intentions). For instance you may want money but the feeling or essence of what you want is freedom, security, safety, etc.

Such as:

- **Life Partnership Intentions:**
  o I intend to feel loved and loving in my relationship with _____
  o I intend for us to both feel respected, honored and supported by each other
  o I intend for us to have fun together
  o I intend for us to always remember the love, no matter what challenges or opportunities we face

- **Other Relationships Intentions:**
  o I intend to feel grateful for all the relationships in my life
  o I intend to love unconditionally as much as I am capable
  o I intend to have compassion for others in my life
  o I intend to create opportunities for connectedness to all who enter my life
  o I intend to have fun with other people in every way possible

- **Work Intentions:**
  o I intend to love my job

o I intend to work at a job where I feel excited, prosperous, joyful and creative!

- **Physical Body Intentions:**
  o I intend to feel healthy, vibrant, beautiful and toned
  o I intend to allow my body to move gracefully and naturally to the ideal weight for my body
  o I intend to love my body

- **Physical Surroundings Intentions:**
  o I intend to have a home in which I feel at peace, safe and secure, both day and night
  o I intend to love my home
  o I intend to live in a home that feels spacious, loving, joyous, beautiful, nurturing, creative and supportive
  o I intend to live in a home surrounded by homes, people and businesses of similar energies

- **Mental and Emotional Intentions:**
  o I intend to feel patient
  o I intend to feel happy
  o I intend to be conscious and awake and intentional about how I spend my time and mental, emotional, physical and

spiritual resources

o I intend to feel passionate about my life

- **Financial Intentions:**
  - o I intend to feel absolutely abundant
  - o I intend to always feel secure in knowing I will have more than enough money to do all I dream of doing

- **Lifestyle Intentions:**
  - o I intend to feel excited and passionate about my life, my hobbies and my lifestyle including but not limited to travel to foreign countries

☐ **Ask for help** in manifesting your intentions, and open to the possibility that your unseen friends may have an even grander dream for you.

You may want to add:

"I request and intend to receive help from all of my unseen friends to manifest all of my intentions even greater than stated, with harm to none."

Congratulations! You are on your way to a life you love!

APPENDIX B

A LETTER FROM YOUR FUTURE SELF

Read this letter from your future self as a way to tap into the resonance of what your life will be like when you have the dream. Feel free t o change this letter to feel/sound more like yourself.

Dear _____,

This is your future self, writing this letter. I wanted you to know what it is like to live the life you always dreamed of.

Well, in one word, it is *fabulous*!

Did all of your intentions come true? Well, maybe they don't *look* the way you might have pictured them. But the essence *did* manifest...on every last one of them (and some of them turned out so much better than you'd even imagined)! Oh... it is wonderful.

Life is very sweet right now. Worry and doubt have become things of the past. I enjoy every minute of every day, savoring the moments with my friends and family, my work, my hobbies and myself.

The abundance and prosperity that have filled my life were easier to create than I ever imagined. And the love, oh the love...it is more wonderful than I ever dreamed.

I move through my life with such peace now. I have learned to trust myself and my universe. Knowing I am always safe and can always create what I want allows for a beautiful calm and sense of safety that I never knew existed.

I love and respect what I have created. I take better care of my body, my loved ones and even my things. I am grateful for everything in my life.

I feel joy, love and satisfaction with my world all of the time now.

You are going to love it here! (And a little advice...if you feel these feelings now, you will get here even sooner than I did!)

With love,

Your Future Self

A note from Boni: For weekly messages from your unseen friends, delivered to your inbox, visit: http://www.livealifeyoulove. com/email-sign-up/

APPENDIX C

REQUESTS TO YOUR HIGHER SELF

Use these requests to your higher self as a preface and closing when you sit down to work on your dream.

Invitation to Assist

Dear higher self, please help me with the work I am about to do. I ask for your help with my dream and the process of manifesting it. I ask for your assistance with clarity, insight, trust and focus. Thank you.

Closing with Gratitude

Dear higher self, thank you for your assistance this day. I ask that you continue to assist me, and gently help me to be aware of my thoughts, discover my beliefs, recognize my patterns and to stay in joy this day and every day. Thank you.

ACKNOWLEDGMENTS

Although bringing this book into being required many hours alone at my keyboard, I've never been involved in a project that was more of a "team effort" than this one. And yes, many of those on *The Map* "team" are my non-physical, unseen friends. However, this book would not exist without their steadfast guidance, love and commitment to me and this work. And although they probably couldn't care less whether they are publicly acknowledged, they, above all, deserve my undying gratitude.

I also enjoyed great support from people with actual physical bodies, including my wonderful editor, Colleen Mauro, who was instrumental in coaxing the book out of me and helped to shape it into its final form. Special thanks go to Hal Zina Bennett, who encouraged my writing for years and helped in the process to name *The Map*. I am also grateful to Doug

Belscher, the book's guardian on the road to publishing, and Carla Johnson, who read the book aloud to me in its entirety, giving me the opportunity to hear its words from a voice outside my head. I must also acknowledge the Inner Art Inc. team, including Sara Blette, Gwen Buehler, Heidi Wattier and Jessica Anderson. I thank them all for their help, support and belief in me and *The Map*.

I am also immensely grateful for the teachers and guides I have worked with over the years who have taught me much of what I know about conscious creation and spirituality. Although there have been *many* who have had positive impact on my life, and I'm grateful for each and every one of them, there are a few who deserve special thanks:

Lazaris,[1] a non-physical entity channeled through Jach Pursel, is a teacher and friend with whom I believe I planned on working long before I became physical this lifetime. I have had the pleasure of learning and growing with Lazaris since 1989, and the impact his love, wisdom and healing has had on my life is absolutely and totally beyond words. The gratitude I feel for what Lazaris has meant to me throughout my lifetime is immense. I will never be able to express the deep meaning, healing and love that he brought into my life.

I am also deeply indebted to another channeled group with whom I have worked nearly weekly since 2006. The Team,[2]

---

1   www.lazaris.com

2   www.ethealing.com

channeled by Jackie Salvitti, has helped me to heal, grow and dream bigger dreams (not to mention manifest those dreams) in ways beyond the scope of (even my fairly sizable) imagination. To them, also, my deepest gratitude.

And Galexis,[3] another group of non-physical entities, channeled through Ginger Chalford Metraux, has also been a huge source of support, clarity and guidance in my long and sometimes bumpy path of growth. I have worked with Galexis on a regular basis since 1995, and I will be forever grateful for their impact on my life and in my world, via their gentle and patient guidance.

To my sons, Brandon and Brett, I thank you for all of the wonderful opportunities you have given me to grow and to love. And to my wonderful magician husband, Richard Schaden, goes a world of thanks for your never-ending love, support and belief in me and my work. It never would have happened without you.

And to my magical readers, thank you...and Namaste.

---

3   www.galexisspirit.com

Made in the USA
San Bernardino, CA
01 December 2013